WOMAN

Good Luck and Prosperity in everything you do!

Alanna! You are a blessing.

WOMAN

a memoir by

Veemala Victoria Persaud

urlink
PRINT & MEDIA

1603 Capitol Ave., Suite 310 Cheyenne, Wyoming USA 82001
1-888-980-6523 | admin@urlinkpublishing.com

URLink Print and Media is committed to excellence in the publishing industry.

Published in the United States of America
ISBN 978-1-64367-898-6 (Paperback)
ISBN 978-1-64367-897-9 (Digital)

Non-Fiction
26.09.19

DEDICATION

Reflecting with sadness on a once imprisoned soul, a long list of tortured memories arises.

> I PRAY, DEAR LORD ALMIGHTY, FORGIVE THE ONES WHO HAVE SINNED AGAINST ME, BUT MOST OF ALL, I BEG YOUR FORGIVENESS FOR ANY AND ALL MY TRANSGRESSIONS ONTO OTHERS. I PRAY FOR THE INNOCENT AND ASK THAT YOU PROTECT THEM FROM REPEATING ANY UNBECOMING BEHAVIORS THAT ARE. I HUMBLY BESEECH YOU. AMEN.

All of my love to Mom and my beloved siblings. I love you!

ACKNOWLEDGMENTS

To all who have crossed my path, I would like to give honor, respect, and thanks to all that you have done for me. Your support and effort have helped me to build strength as I have exceeded the possibilities of love. To my mother, grandmother and family; I owe you my due diligence for sticking by my side through the ins and outs of my journey. The love you give reaches to the depths of my heart. To all the friends I have encountered, thank you as well. Please know that so much of my uprising would not have been without you.

Thanks and Love.

CONTENTS

PREFACE

I wanted the title of this book to greatly impact and inspire those who may need courage in their own lives. This book, *Wo-Man*, was written for those in similar predicaments who may need a boost of encouragement, support, and hope. Perhaps those individuals who read the many stories to follow will come to know that they are more capable and more powerful than they believe. My motivation in setting all this down on paper, in speaking out, has been to help liberate all those who have endured trauma and pain as they survived the best they could from childhood to adulthood. This book is a collection of my life's extreme moments (extreme fear, sorrow, extreme joy) and of the people who touched my life. My life from its very beginning up until the present has been a wild rollercoaster ride. While writing this book I have journeyed through a landscape of memories and events that I had not always accepted or conquered. I hope it serves as a validation and source of comfort to all those facing and conquering their demons.

INTRODUCTION

From chaos to success, this is a story of the violence and abuse I have endured. It talks about a battle of identity, sex, pain, and pleasure. I am still alive; alive to share my story and to encourage others. Hopefully my story will help others avoid the pain and torture that I have miraculously survived.

The feelings and emotions within each story may cause the reader to wince, grimace, and even weep in empathy. My feelings are a smorgasbord, ranging from desperation to delight. My self-imposed mission to reveal the truth requires the depiction of each and every one of these shades of emotion.

Every day I remain tortured; you will see. I, Veemala, have inflicted deep, dark hurt on others—but never intentionally. My heart is heavy, pulled down not by the violations of body and spirit I have suffered but also by the knowledge of the undeniable pain I have inflicted on innocent and blameless others.

As you read my story, try not to judge. Wait until the conclusion of my memoir. Then and only then can you decide!

Fact: Bananas are one of the healthiest fruits, chock full of vitamins and minerals. They are often enjoyed in shakes, as part of a meal, or as a dessert—the way nature intended.

Nature never intended bananas to be shoved sadistically down a throat.

Imagine: four whole bananas suffocating you, choking you. Although you cannot breathe, you must not cry, must not break. *Impossible to imagine*, you might think.

All the while, they laughed.

All I could think about…wrap my mind around…was *Breathe Veemala, breathe! Hold on…Fight!…even if only in your mind.*

That was my mantra: *Win, you must win.*

My mind urging my body to block the physical pain. I promise my almost lifeless body that there is hope; that there may be a better life ahead.

I emerged from these atrocities with questions.

Who am I?

Which one of the selves that I have created is the real me?

Should I conform to society's "norms?"

Or can I truly be me?

Is there anyone out there for me?

Someone who will really care?

Someone who will understand me?

Someone who will accept me? Really and truly accept me?

My young, undeveloped mind could not grasp what was happening.

Why me? Why is it always me?

CHAPTER 1

Misery Always Waiting

In 1988, I was eleven years old. Eleven years old with a flock of butterflies fluttering in my stomach. Sometimes it felt like boiling acid. I was a worried soul.

What should I do?

How do I escape from this perpetual agitation?

"Ahhhh, ahhhh!" always screaming from the inside. That's how it felt: *agony.* Would the agony ever heal—or would it go on forever?

I was searching for inner peace, for serenity, but it always fled, just beyond my reach, running from me. That feeling again! It would not stop!

Oh no!

Dear Big Spirit in the sky, please don't let it happen again. Please!

I had to hide.

Father in Heaven, God (that is what my Mommy calls you), can you make me disappear? *Please?*

The silence was shattered. BAM! BAM! CRASH!...the sound of pots, pans, and dishes smashed and thrown to the ground.

"Nadira! Nadira!"

That was dad. He was home.

Please, Father God, can you save my mommy from him? Then a long, deafening silence…

Pain was in the air. Everyone could feel it. Our house of pain. Next, I heard a low, scornful whimpering followed by wailing and a loud cry. An unmistakable cry of anguish and defeat.

It was Mommy, pleading desperately for mercy. It was her cry for mercy as my dad smashed her head one time and then another against the kitchen's brick wall. I thought he would never stop.

Our house was about 1,000 square feet in size, with two bedrooms. There was no place to hide.

He slammed his fist into her breast, with hard and swift brutal punches. He was pummeling her body, using his fists and feet like some unstoppable motor out of control. Finally, she passed out from the pain. This was a moment I would never forget.

It was an uneven match; tiny David pitted against Goliath. My six-foot-tall father towered over my mother, who was a good foot shorter. He weighed at least twice as much as her and along with his height and ferocity, used that to his advantage, taking my mother down.

I could ignore the evidence of my senses. Where was God? What was this called?

I remember thinking, *You must not cry. You have to be strong.* I can still hear his maddened voice echoing in my head, "YOU ARE A CURSE! I DON'T WANT SUCH A CURSE IN MY HOUSE."

I was five years old and living in a third world country; my undeveloped child's mind had no idea of what I was supposed to do. No idea of what 'behaving' a certain way meant. Nor how these scenes of violence and battery would later impact my life. The worst moments in my life stood out most prominently, overshadowing the good ones.

Has anyone ever questioned why?

Does the pain outlast all the other feelings--or is life just set up this way?

RING, RING! RING!

Darn! It was the phone. I must have overslept.

What time was it?

"Hello...Hi, old lady." (It was grandmother, from my mother's side. I liked teasing her that way). "Why are you calling me this early," I asked, pretending to be annoyed.

"Well, I wanted to remind you that I'm coming over to get a haircut. Get to the salon before your real clients show up. Were you still asleep? My goodness, child, it's almost 8:00 AM.

I hesitated before responding. "It's OK, no problem! I was having a terrible dream. Actually, I'm glad you woke me up."

"Hmm," she muttered, "still getting those nightmares? Please take my advice: get some professional help."

After a slight pause, I answered. "Yes, old lady, I've already made an appointment for later today. Come by in a half-hour so I can do your hair before my first client arrives."

"OK love," she said. "I am walking over now. I should be there soon."

My grandma now lives about five blocks away with my aunt. She migrated here many years ago.

CHAPTER 2

Therapy

DAYDREAMING ON THE TRAIN RIDE to my appointment is not a good idea. Given my taste for escaping reality into fantasy, I could end up miles away before realizing I had missed my stop.

I was in my late 20's, a passenger on the 'A' train from Queens, New York. The click and static of the intercom, and the conductor's voice announcing our approaching destination brought me back to reality. For a very brief moment, I had slipped back into my make-believe world. I love it there. Make-believe Land is my only escape; the only place my soul finds peace and freedom. Peace and freedom from the deep scars, temporary respite from the pain and the unimaginable horrors of the past.

"Ma'am...ma'am?"

I was quickly brought back to reality by the sound of the receptionist's voice. She was addressing me.

"Oh, hi," I said. I managed a quick smile. "I'm here to see Dr. Irene."

"And your name?"

"It's Veemala," I answered. "Sorry, I thought I had mentioned that."

She gave me a quizzical look which made me very self-conscious. Being self-conscious was my baseline and something that I had been struggling with all of my life. Searching for my identity. The receptionist's question made me even *more* self-conscious.

"Please be seated. I'll let you know when it's your turn," she told me. She continued to give me that questionable look as I walked towards my seat. I could feel her eyes on my back.

I had to refresh my make-up before seeing the therapist. I pulled out my make-up case (something I am never without), staring at my reflection in the compact's tiny mirror. I was horrified at what I saw: long, dark streaks of mascara from my eyes, and blotches of my natural skin tone peeking through my otherwise carefully made-up face.

"Ha!" That was my own voice, laughing at me in amusement and derision. No wonder the receptionist kept staring at me like that!

I had been so engulfed by sorrow, so overwhelmed by the past while riding the train that I did not even realize I was weeping, flooding my face with tears. After so many moments like this, I firmly resolved to forgive myself for reverting back to childhood.

Oh well, too late!

"Veemala?"

I heard my name and stood up. Dr. Irene reached her hand out to welcome me.

"I am Dr. Irene. This way, please."

CHAPTER 3

Conversation With Dr. Irene

The room was small, not quite how I had envisioned it. I was expecting something much larger in scale, a contemporary space replete with high ceiling, big wide windows, and low comfortable couches…Not!

How silly of me.

From the moment I landed in the States (arriving at Miami International Airport in 2003), I felt I had touched down in a daydream, in a (good) fantasy land filled with bright lights, towering skyscrapers, millions of cars, buses, trains, and planes.

This land was waiting to embrace me. It freed me from the dark clutches of violent savagery and trembling fear of the people and country I once knew.

"I see you were referred by Dr. Zhao?" she asked. "And what kind of treatment do you think you need?"

Suddenly, I was drawn back from my dark thoughts to the miraculous present.

"What? Oh, I'm sorry," I apologized. Would there ever come a time when I didn't need to instinctively *apologize*? "Well, Dr. Zhao feels that I should get help for all the things that have affected my life. You see, I'm not who you think I am... but I am really me." I offered what seemed like confused words by way of explanation.

The words flowed from my mouth like water from a burst dam.

"I have two brothers and one sister. I am the oldest. I am originally from Guyana, which is the only English-speaking country in South America. My country had been colonized by the British, and my ancestors came there from India. "They were brought there as indentured slaves, along with Africans, Chinese, Amerindians, Portuguese and Europeans. Guyana gained its independence in 1966 and, ever since, the country has had massive political problems."

I wanted to yell out to the world, wanted everyone to know about all the indignities and violence I had endured in forced silence for so many years. However, Dr. Irene gently placed her hands on my shoulder, stopping me in mid-sentence.

"Veemala," she said, "it's alright. Let me explain how it works. Much as you might want to, you can't cover over 30 years of life experience in one 30-minute sitting! Suppose we set you up with a schedule of some 30-minute sessions for three weeks or so. At that point, with a better idea of your issues, we will re-evaluate the situation, perhaps set you up with psychiatrist. Would you like something to drink?"

I shook my head "no," and she suggested that I get a little more comfortable. She indicated another chair that was wider and lower, right beside the gentle muted light of a small table lamp.

I welcomed the suggestion. It was a great one. I felt comfortable and protected, as though I were in a cocoon.

Dr. Irene offered some warm tea, which I gladly accepted. It tasted great- almost soothing!

Dr. Irene ignored the rapid knocking on the door. She simply didn't respond. Then the phone rang. She answered it.

Shortly after this, she left the room but quickly returned, taking a package from her desk as she apologized, asking me to make myself comfortable. She would be back shortly.

I felt so comfortable and so protected. Soon enough I drifted into a light doze. Hmm…this was good. *I needed this.*

I had not felt this way since - ever. It was a sweet moment, and I lingered there. *Being in the moment* was like sitting on a beach caressed by a soft summer breeze.

CHAPTER 4

Seeking A Savior

AT AGE 10--YES, I AM 10 years old now, but was there any difference from five years before?

Nothing had changed. It all felt the same.

The only thing that changed was the day; nothing different in the moment, nothing in the action of the others around me.

If only they would let me play with them like all the other children do. If only I could walk or run to places like others do. If only my brain could figure a way out, how to fix things, how to convince them, how to explain it all.

Imagine waking up every day in a prison. A prison with no guards, no parole, and no release date. There is just one inmate – you.

The prison? My body was the prison, trapping the real me inside. The me I desperately wanted to be but could not. Whenever I tried to get out, the others would push me back in or attack me for being different.

No love for me inside this prison without walls; and no love for me at home.

If only love could live in our house.

What if love did live in our house? Would life be any better? Would it?

"Vishal! And Veemala! Come on, hurry up, we have to run! He is going to kill us!"

I hear the sharpening of the machete. I hear him say it.

"Tonight I'm going to slice you up into pieces."

Why was my dad doing this, threatening to cut my mummy up into pieces?

Why?

"Dear God..."

Oh yes, now that I am older, I know His name. At five years old, I thought of him as the Great Spirit in the sky. My mother had a different name for him: our loving Father God.

Odd, how I am able to process all of this in one frightening moment. Why is my mind constantly on a roll? Why the constant rain in my heart?

I envisioned a future of mindlessly repeating every action, every terror-soaked gesture that my mom performed with well-practiced ease. My life seemed hellbent toward a depressive frenzy.

In my opinion, no child should have to see or hear such things. No wonder the world is the way it is today; no wonder the high rates of child suicide. Why should any child be driven to destroy him or herself?

There is terror and cruelty and evil in this world. Some speculate that somehow, someday, a change will come. But they are ultimately more concerned with the "real" issues: the bills they have to pay, the anger that screams for release, the thirst for alcohol; not the hearts of the little ones...a little one like me.

My brother and I were left out, excluded. We might as well have been invisible. Saying those prayers was my only outlet. Over time they grew old, like all things in life, and still, we needed to be saved.

CHAPTER 5

A Small Step Towards Freedom

IT WAS JUST PAST 8:00 AM and my mother gently woke my brother and me. Mom was thin and petite, with long lustrous brown hair. My brother was a year younger than me and very brave for his age.

"It's time to go back to the house and pack our things," our mom said. "Your father has already left for work, and that gives us enough time to get out. We are going to stay with your grandmother."

We were seeking shelter at our mother's mother. I still hear the sounds from last night, my father sharpening the machete and threatening our mother's life.

By now, our neighbors were all accustomed to hearing the screams of agony that habitually came from our house. They were well aware of the brutal beatings our mother had to endure at the hands of our alcoholic father.

Why didn't anyone say something? Or call for help? Why didn't anyone step in?

They could have easily intervened. There were dozens, if not hundreds of opportunities. Anyone could have called someone for help, but no one did. We always had to go to them, pleading for refuge.

Spending the night at the neighbor's, and hiding from our father's alcohol-fueled rage became the norm.

My mother thanked our neighbor for the shelter we received, and we walked hurriedly back towards our small house. They knew what was happening, but all they did was help us to hide.

I guess that was better than nothing.

I am so excited that we would not be coming back to this house, a house full of distress, a house that cries and groans… just like my mommy does when her head is being beaten into the wall by my dad.

"Oh, God! Please stop those horrible sounds from echoing in my head."

The slaps, punches, and beatings I witnessed have been eating away at my brain. The sight of my poor mother's limp body has become a torment to my soul.

"Vemeela!"

I hear my younger brother calling me as I stand daydreaming in the hallway of our house. I was, for a moment, excited. Finally, we were leaving, running away from daddy, but I am sad, too.

Why do I feel sad? For whom am I sad? I had no friends. That's right: NO FRIENDS, not in my small neighborhood and most definitely not at school.

I was about to walk past the spot in the living room where my dad usually sat when I suddenly froze.

"No! No!" I cried out loud, as I placed my unusually small hands over my ears to try and block out the thought that was crossing my mind. *It's true, it's all true, but why do I want to block it out?* How could I have forgotten this? How?

Only old people forget things, not young ones like me. That is what mom always said.

The vision in my head was vivid. I saw my dad hugging me tightly, tears flooding his eyes and streaming down his face. The words he spoke touched me. His words touch me even now as I reflect back on that scene in my head. My dad loves me, yes, he truly loves. Why am I sure?

Because he said it to me.

Yes, my dad cried and said that he truly loves me. Why did I not remember that? Why?

I love my dad, too.

But why am I invisible to him when there are friends and family around? Why?

Once again, my brother's voice interrupted my thoughts, moving me to action.

"Veemala, Ma wants us to help her pack," he said. "Hurry up."

"I'm coming. I'm coming! Stop calling me," I shouted back to him, upset that he had disturbed my daydream.

CHAPTER 6

We Move In

ARRIVING AT MY GRANDMOTHER'S HOUSE that day was a big relief for me.

No more unjustified beatings from my father. (Are beatings ever justified?) The end of my mother running and hiding in fear. No longer do I have to watch in horror as my brave younger brother tries to step in and stop the beatings.

I was released from the prison that was my father's house. No longer would I have to cower away from the sad, disdainful stares from the man I called Daddy. I was safe now.

Was I?

I stood in my grandmother's house listening to the chatter of the older family members. They were talking excitedly about our arrival, planning who was going to sleep where. My grandmother did not live alone. Another of her six daughters and her family - my aunt, her husband, and their two children - lived there too. These cousins were around the same age as my brother and me.

The whole clan lived in a small, three-bedroom house. I knew that things were going to be much different from usual, but I didn't know how.

I didn't fully understand it, but my heart felt lighter. Some of the weight of the sorrow and fear of our own house lifted. Blessed relief! Now my mom would smile - smile at me - more.

I was so happy! I loved when my mom hugged and comforted me. I felt like nothing could harm me with my brave mother - the brave mother hen - protecting her young.

I craved that love each moment of my life. And who would not?

I wished moments like those would spring up like blooming flowers, regularly, predictably, forever. My daydreams and my fantasy world were too often unrealizable, unrealistic. Clinging to dreams that might never come true was a regular habit of mine.

Dad, oh, Dad!

I was hoping a day would arrive when he would turn over a new leaf, and we would have a normal happy family. Decency and order would preside, but that was just another impossible dream.

We were like runaway slaves, having to escape from our own father. I am sure my mother thanked God for this respite from hopelessness and the nights of beatings.

Staying one day longer could have ended her life.

It is 1989. We had been living with my grandmother and cousins for a year. I was 11 years old.

All of us lived together under one roof. Most of our belongings remained unpacked, and there was no privacy. My grandmother's house was located in the county of Essequibo, an agricultural area that was also home to our country's largest river. We lived on top of one another. Having enough money or food to eat were my mother's greatest worries. She needed to feed us and provide our material needs though she had never worked outside the home. We lived on the pittance doled out to her by my dad on an irregular, infrequent basis.

My dad spent most of his money on drink. We were free from dad's physical and emotional abuse, but we suffered terribly from financial privation. It was nearly impossible to get by.

Living in this overcrowded, underfed household was becoming unbearable. My mother looked for work.

Guyana was mostly wilderness. The water supply was affected by the sewage and toxic chemicals spewing forth from the factories.

Guyana sits on the northeast coach of South America, close to the Caribbean Sea. Venezuela, Brazil, and Surinam are its neighbors.

Most of Guyana's population were poor - just like us. Guyana, a third world country, was ranked the poorest in all of South America.

You can see and read about the struggle my mother and those around us went through. In a *Travel GC* article, one author described our country like this: Crime is prevalent across Guyana. Assaults, break-ins, armed robberies, pickpocketing, purse snatching, theft from cars, and carjacking are all common. Be particularly cautious in the Georgetown areas of Stabroek Market, Tiger Bay, and south of Brickdam Street. Criminals prefer to target foreigners and returning Guyanese citizens.

Sadly enough, his observations were true. Only the strong survive in Guyana. I attribute my survival to sheer luck. We were not the only family struggling to stay alive. Other children walked the streets too.

There were no safe places for children in Guyana-- especially for a child like me.

CHAPTER 7

School of Hard Knocks

How SLOWLY A YEAR GOES by when the one person you love and rely on exits your world. No reason, no excuse in the world was justification enough to soothe my pain, not even the fact that we had saved my mom from my drunken homicidal dad.

One year in my life felt like a million. I was in a torture cell filled with nails and thorns, built for me alone. I was terrified that I would stop breathing, so I could almost never fall asleep. I dreaded the dreams and nightmares that exploded every night in my brain.

The single exception was school. I loved school. I wanted to learn and fit in. Unfortunately, none of that was in the cards. Life chose a very different path for me.

Mom finally found a job living as a nanny in Venezuela. The boat she will travel on leaves tomorrow morning at 6:45 AM, which means she would be leaving my grandmother's house at four. Another piece of my life is slipping from the pitiful grasp of our hands.

We would have to raise ourselves.

I see myself with my head spinning and unable to contain my tears. I am on the receiving end of nasty stares and rude suggestions from the rest of the family.

"Shut up!" they yell. "Stop crying!"

"You need to be brave now," they said later. My inner self screamed for help.

"Veemala, can you take me back to where you said your dad never wanted to give you attention when the rest of the family or friends were around?"

"Veemala...are you awake? Veemala?"

What?

I must have fallen asleep. I didn't hear Dr. Irene entering the room.

What was she saying?

How embarrassing. How long had I been sleeping?

What should my answer be?

"I am dreadfully sorry, Doctor. I must have dozed off," I said. "If you could tell me where you buy that tea I just drank I'm sure my nights would be much more bearable."

I was rambling and practically babbling, afraid to stop talking. Afraid I might have said something embarrassing while asleep.

Wait a minute...that's why I'm here...to get some help, some relief from the nightmares.

Overthinking and endless worry were my daily tonic. Clearly, it was showing. *OK Veemala, relax. Nothing to fear here*, I told myself. I couldn't help viewing everything in my life as worthless, unlovable, dejected, and lost.

"You were asleep for a good part of the hour, but you have shared quite a bit," Dr. Irene explained. "You are so filled with pain that each time you close your eyes, your mouth opens up and some of that pain comes spilling out."

I sat staring at the kind doctor, wondering how much I might have said.

"We will begin where we left off, same time next week, OK?" she remarked. "Oh, would you like to take home a few packets of that tea?"

I accepted the offer gladly. I might even get a decent night's sleep.

Walking to the train station, I felt some relief: a slight reprieve, which was a blessing, some respite from the tension and hurt I always feel. Usually I have an uncomfortable feeling in my chest.

No doubt about it: sharing is good.

Tea in hand, I boarded the train for Queens. Destination: home.

Who can foresee the future? Who could imagine the infinite fear I am about to disclose?

CHAPTER 8

Farewell, Mother

"I AM ONLY DOING THIS to make life better for you and your brother," my mother explained. "I won't be gone for long. You see how hard life is for us like this? I love you and your brother very much. It won't be long, just a couple of months, OK?"

My mother's voice kept playing in my head: "I love you. I will be back soon."

Her words painted the walls of my ears.

Then it was morning, much too soon.

She hugged us, told us to behave, and repeated that she loved us. I cried uncontrollably.

My brother cried, too, but not the way I did. He was always in better control of his emotions. It had not been a full three hours since our mother had gone that my life became a downward spiral towards a destiny I did not choose, a destiny brutally forced upon me.

This house had become another prison just like my father's house before. Granted, there was no Goliath threatening to crush us. But now, without my mother, there was nobody to care for us. My brother and I would be treated like servants, unloved lackeys of my aunt and uncle, and there was nothing we could do about it.

"Veemala!"

Hearing my name in this new empty hell sent shivers down my spine. The sadness of my mother's departure weighed heavily on my heart and soul.

"Coming," was my weak response. Sheer pressure made it difficult to speak.

I kept replaying the words of a sad song in my head, *"When will I see you again, Will I have to suffer and struggle forever?"*

I made up some of the words, but it was my song; my private song of pain.

As I wiped at my tear-stained face, I prepared myself for what was to come. My aunt stood by the back door watching me as I emerged from the outdoor toilet, the latrine. The latrine became the crying place for my overburdened heart.

"Child, hurry up! Almost seven o'clock and you need to take the cows and goats out to pasture." The pasture was about a half-mile from the house.

"When you are done, you will need to wash out these diapers and hang them on the line to dry. And don't let them touch the ground! Hurry, if you want to go to school."

My heart skipped several beats. *Why, why, why?*

"Yes, auntie, I'm coming."

I was never afraid of animals, and it was quite easy for me to lead the cows and goats to pasture. At first, I was even excited about being in control of *something* in my life. However, after the first two or three days of trudging through slushy mud and cow manure, it got old very fast. The chores got to me in the worst possible way.

It was exhausting running after the cows and goats as I tried to bring them in line with the rest of the herd. On many occasions, one or more of them took off in different directions - usually in opposite directions - and then I'd be late for school.

I was always late for school.

I can barely recall what I ate for breakfast. A quick grab at a cup of black tea and a small bun or a slice of buttered bread was my portion. I dared not ask for more.

That is how I came to feel. When the hunger pangs hit me hard, I kept thinking about my mom, about how much she loved me. There was enough food - enough food for all - just not for me.

I watched my cousins stuff their faces. I watched as they tossed their leftovers to the dogs and chickens in the yard. I watched as auntie Bee and her husband spoiled my cousins with love.

They got everything they asked for - and then some. They played for long hours outdoors with their friends. They were encouraged to get their school work done before bed. They got to choose the best fruits and enjoyed the comfort of their beds. Not me! I had to sleep on the floor. I never had free time to recover from the hard days of many unreasonable chores. Fun or enjoyment was completely out of the question.

Hugs and kisses were necessities I could only dream of. I watched with envy as my cousins were showered with hugs and kisses, with embraces from my grandmother and their parents. The only time I ever got them were in fantasies.

I daydream a lot.

I daydream while walking the cattle to and from the pasture. I daydream on my way to school and in I daydream in school.

Such dreams! I see myself in beautiful clothing, in ballrooms, moving graciously and being admired by elegant men and women. There are times when I could almost taste the rich, decadent meals piled high on large oaken tables.

In my head, I am complete and happy - almost euphoric. Without these fantasies I have nothing. I am nothing.

I feel so alone. I have a brother, but my mom is in another country, very far away. Oh, I almost forgot. I have a dad.

I still feel like a motherless child: yes, an orphan.

I think it might rain. I hate it when the clouds are dark and unrevealing, but the rain I love. Walking in the rain with my thoughts and fantasies; no one to disturb or distract me from fantasies that only I could dream of, and hope would one day come true!

Standing behind my grandmother, I feel the darkness of the clouds entering my soul. It gives me chills. I get feelings I have never had before.

Suddenly a loud boom! It is the sound of thunder, from which I recoil in fear.

Simultaneously, I heard auntie's husband telling me to go outside.

"Get the animals! It's going to rain hard, and I don't want them to get soaked."

Then he walks away.

CHAPTER 9

The Beginning Of Many Storms

It was dark, wet, and cold as I hurried along the narrow, uneven path towards the pasture for the animals. Today was very different. I could feel it in my bones; the fear of what lay ahead. That day I learned that my gut feeling or my intuition was never wrong.

But I had to do my chores.

So off I went. I entered the pasture about 50 yards or so from the field where the cows and goats were moving restlessly. That's when I saw a dark shadow emerging from the shaded cover of a tree.

Who was there?

It was too early; still too dark and wet for anyone to be out here - except me, of course. The shadow was approaching me, and I felt my throat go dry. Waves of nervous heat radiated from my forehead. Even in the cold and rain I could still feel the heat.

I was paralyzed with fear, trying to think of some way to protect myself, but I was so frightened that I could not think straight.

The shadow spoke. "I know what you are," he said, as he moved closer and closer toward me. "And I want some sex."

My voice sounded like someone else's voice, echoing from very far away.

"No, no, leave me alone," I pleaded.

But I was weak from fear, and my throat was parched. If only someone would come along and save me. Just show up and interrupt this nightmare.

Suddenly, his hands were on my body. I struggled to back away from him, trying my best to shout or scream.

But no sound came from my dry desert throat. I was paralyzed by fear.

The monster slammed my frail body against a tree; his arms locked tight around me. I was small and frail, and he had me in his grip. After moving to my grandmother's house my physical appearance and mental stability declined. I was now a very skinny, fragile child, thanks to the extremely hard daily labor and the meager portions of food thrown my way.

Malnourished, deprived of all human affection, I looked different. I was an outcast; some kind of alien or freak.

I tried to fight, but I was no match for that man, the monster who was attacking me, taking me down. He molested me, his rough, gnarled fingers ripping into my flesh, choking my neck as he forced his hands down between my legs to paw at my privates.

It was then that he began to grunt, nearly incomprehensible barks and commands.

"I KNOW YOU WANT IT. TAKE IT. TELL ME HOW MUCH YOU NEED IT. OH, YES, TELL ME. TAKE IT. LET ME GIVE IT TO YOU GOOD. DON'T FIGHT BACK BECAUSE NO ONE IS HERE BUT US."

As he slammed my slight body to the ground, my mind floated in the air somewhere above me. It watched with horror as the monster attacked me in the most shocking and gruesome way possible.

He tugged, dragged, and ripped my clothes from my body as I begged and pleaded for him to stop. I knew the whole time that it was hopeless. The ground was hard and cruel against my flesh, like the nasty, soulless man forcing me down. His weight on top of me made it impossible to escape.

He penetrated me. The sudden, shocking pain; the assault on my body and private parts were like death to me. He ravaged my anus, and I prayed to die.

I prayed to die; prayed for the earth to open and swallow me up. That would have been best. He slammed himself into my body repeatedly, thrusting in and out again and again, deeper and harder.

At some point, I must have passed out from the combined terror and pain. The sexual assault was ferocious, bestial. When I did wake, this predator was violating my innards with his massive member. I was darting in and out of consciousness but then noticed through my tears a second figure looming over us.

It was another man.

I felt a flicker of hope. Was someone there to save me? No, I was so wrong.

I quickly spotted the unnatural, strange excitement in the eyes of this stranger, and I knew that life for me was over. My frail body would be unable to endure a double assault.

The stranger spoke to my assailant.

"You know, I have to get a turn too if I'm not going to tell," he glibly joked with my attacker.

I could see the dark sky, the rain blinding my tear-filled eyes. The trees shook with the wind blowing in hatred towards the earth; the earth upon which I was brutally raped.

My assailant pulled out of my body and laughed.

"Sure man, go ahead, take your turn," he said to the newcomer. "It's going to be our little secret."

My mind went blank, and my body numb. I must have died for an hour. That's how it felt. I regained consciousness to find both my assailants standing there smiling at each other.

I struggled to put my clothes on as they helped me. I blurted out that I was going to tell my family.

That only made them laugh hysterically.

"Go ahead, no one will believe you," one of them said to me, laughing more uproariously. "And if you do, then everyone will know what you are, and you will bring shame on yourself and your family."

As they walked away, I could hear them laughing like two pals sharing a good joke. I saw them threatening and sneering at me. They were two cousins who lived four houses away from us. They were supposed to be decent Christian boys, upstanding models for the community, but they sure proved how indecent and irreligious they were.

They were in their twenties, about 5 feet 10 inches tall. They sang in the church choir and assisted with baptisms in the local Christian church. It was going to be my word against theirs. Who would protect me anyway? All I could focus on was death. I wanted to die. I wanted the earth to burst and take me down.

I cannot recall how I got back home, but I do recall that my aunt demanded explanations from me. Why was I late? How did my clothes become torn? It was dark and wet and stormy. The power and lights were out. In the darkness, still in a daze, I considered a dozen possible explanations. Finally, I told her that I fell and my clothes got caught on the pasture's barbed-wire fence while getting one of the cows out from the mud in the pasture.

I guess that was reason enough for her, and so ended our conversation.

That night I fell asleep wracked with pain and sorrow. All I wanted was for the earth to swallow me up. I had been raped, and there was no one to protect me. It hurts.

What would anyone do if I actually talked about it? No one would believe me. They would laugh, especially since I walked, talked, and even acted differently beyond my control.

Our neighbor's son and his cousin had raped me; boys from a strong religious background. I decided to stay quiet and keep it all to myself: *my little secret.*

My brother went back to live with my daddy. Now I was completely alone amidst the circle of my uncaring family. My dad had come back to take me, but my aunt and grandmother convinced him to let me stay with them since I would get a better education. So he left.

My life was useless, ruined. I could not think of anything or anyone. I could not think. I was completely numb and oblivious to the people and the world around me. I was an orphan who craved and cried daily for her mother's return. All I had and lived by was hope.

Two days later, it happened again. My two nemeses, my two rapists were there waiting for me in the pasture.

There was no place to run, nowhere to hide in the wide-open field; the animals were my only witnesses. It was time for my mind and soul to escape, to run for cover to their private hiding place. A place without pain, a place where I could never be found. A place detached from my body, the body that belonged to everyone but me.

So began the almost daily cycle of rape and assault on my body by these two soulless monsters. As time went by, so did the men, from one attacker to another, from one rapist to another.

I started to want it; to welcome my daily violation. I became accustomed to the brutal sex. I actually felt that somehow it healed my pain and sorrow. Many times I even told my attacker that I would be waiting for him there in the pasture.

I created countless fantasies in my head, fantasies that kept me distracted from the curses that plagued my life. The fantasies also served as a distraction from my many chores, chores that began at 5:30 AM and ended late into the night. Each night I laid my weary head down on the hard pillow and collapsed onto the 1-inch mattress they had provided for me on the floor. I was always on the floor. The only way I could fall asleep was imagining that my mother was there, hugging me and rocking me to sleep. Meanwhile, hordes of mosquitoes bit away at me.

My aunt and the rest of the relatives thought little of it, but my daily chores were nothing but child labor from the perspective of the normal world. I always hoped and prayed that I would be in a higher and better place in the future - anywhere better and higher. Those were my hopes that I lived by. Many days I was in my trance, mesmerized by my dreams of power. Being famous was my greatest dream.

CHAPTER 10

A Childhood Robbed

MY NIGHTS WERE SHORT AND sleepless, filled with fears and flashbacks of what I had experienced throughout the day, the week - throughout my whole miserable existence.

I usually woke to the crowing of the cock. It is 5:30 AM and time to rise up and fold up my sleeping items from the floor.

I hear movement in my aunt's room, so I hurry to avoid her scalding accusations that I am late, that I am dragging my feet.

The first thing to do is let the chickens out, a process far more demanding than any desk job could ever be. Farm work is hard work. So is getting along with cows, goats, and chickens without getting harmed. I would scatter the chicken feed on the ground and fill their trays with water.

The pasture where I take the cows and goats is about a half-mile away. I have to move quickly because it can take quite a bit of time getting them there. Animals are strange, and they don't t always cooperate! They don't always move along at the pace you would like. Most times, it takes a lot of effort prodding them along while keeping an eye on the goats, so they don't stray far from the flock.

Some of the cows had to be tethered to a post that was shaded or close to water. In today's society, nobody would dare do such a thing.

I had a great deal of agricultural experience, so being around those animals was like being among friends. Once I was done, it usually took a full 20 minutes or more to return home.

Immediately upon my return, I would have to sweep beneath the house. Unlike here in America, homes in my country are built on stilts that raise them above ground. The ground is bare dirt, not concrete. It was my job to keep it clean, which meant sweeping it at least twice a day.

Even today, Guyana still needs major improvements. The country still faces major issues. I want to be a positive influence, to make things better there, especially for its children. Many live in poverty and poor housing conditions, even as I write this.

One positive note is that the government is finally beginning to focus on the poor. Country housing developments are in the works, and investments into Guyanese communities are being actively encouraged.

Then my grandmother brought a baby cousin home. One of my other aunts gave birth to this cute baby boy whom my grandmother was now going to raise.

Every day there were eight or more diapers to be washed, and as usual, the task fell to me. Washing diapers was very time-consuming. They had to be free of any stains. I had that job for about nine months. Every day I heard the same thing from my aunt or my grandmother as I washed them.

"You need to hurry up with the washing," and "Make sure you get all the stains out. Don't hang them too low on the clothesline."

This was my life, and in life, you have to take things as they are. The family was the priority, and grandma made sure to keep everyone in order, especially before we headed for school.

School starts at 8 AM, and I take a shower outside in the back yard. I quickly swallow the slice of unbuttered bread or pancake, chasing it down with a cold cup of tea or coffee. I grab my school bag and start running along the unpaved street to my school.

The school was also about a half-mile from home, so it took some time to get there. I always barely make it to class, but many days I am late, coming in just as the other kids are about to start writing in their books.

Once there, I find I am breathing hard, trying to recover from the morning chores and all the hassles of the day. Teachers whipped students who were late. I usually got two lashes in the outstretched palms of my hand whenever I was late, which was almost every day, but I was used to it.

I loved school, but the other kids didn't love me. They made it very hard for me. I was teased and bullied and called every ugly word in the book. Processing information was difficult for me because my memory was shot.

I succeeded in school by sheer will power and the grace of the Lord above.

On my way home from school, I always had confusing thoughts. For example, I wondered if I should hurry home to avoid all of the hardcore teasing, tugging, and pushing I had to endure from my peers, or should I drag it out and walk slowly, so I would not have to face the huge amount of work waiting for me at home?

I had no way of avoiding that. No matter how late I arrived home, I had no choice but to do them. Always foremost in my mind was the daily rape by those monsters waiting to ambush me in the pasture.

With all these thoughts swirling in my brain, I finally arrived home from school. After dropping my school bag in a corner and changing into what we call "house clothes," I headed down to my aunt and uncle's farm.

The farm was almost a mile from home - a half-mile beyond the pasture. I always had various things to do depending on the day of the week and on what my uncle had in mind for me that particular day. There was always something to do. I had to fetch firewood and had to clean the trench and pond.

Today was weeding day. I hacked at the weeds and shrubs with a machete. There were many, very overgrown weeds, and they had to be cleared away. I found a batch of little plants placed there by my uncle to remind me to replant them in the same plot where I chopped the weeds.

I was standing, looking at the small plants I had just put in the earth. I was hoping for some time to breathe, for a break from the intense work under the harsh sun when I heard the screech of my uncle's voice.

"Don't just stand there wasting time. You have to water the plants!" he screamed. "Otherwise they will die! Get the bucket, fetch some water from the pond and start wetting them. Now! After that I need you to dig four holes along the fence line. Tomorrow I am going to run barbed wires to keep out the animals."

I hurried away to do as he asked. I did not want to be there alone in the dark. I still had to drive the cows and goats home from the pasture. He was inhuman and heartless. He always treated me so bad.

I am so tired. This is such hard work. Then there was the homework I needed to get done.

I need the strength of a man - three men - to complete these tasks. But my body was only equipped for a woman's work - one woman.

It is 7 PM and I am making my way home, a large bunch of bananas on my head. It feels like 50 pounds, but it may only be 25. A jute bag hung from my shoulder, crammed with vegetables that my uncle wanted me to take back home.

I could barely move with all this weight, but I had to hurry. I still had to get the cattle from the pasture. On tiring days like these I hope and pray that my attackers are not there. Sometimes I actually wanted them to be there so I could feel numb.

On that particular day, I had given up all hope. I didn't even want the attackers to be there. But yes, there they were, ready to pounce.

I am finally home from the pasture with the cattle, broken, battered, and dazed from what my abusers have once again inflicted upon me. It would be a blessing to die now. Nothing in this world will ever bring me joy. Amen.

Faint and practically lifeless, I slowly walked to the chicken coop and leaned my head against the frame. I walked around the coop with a flashlight, counting the chickens to be sure that they were all there.

After that, I forced my arms above my head in order to pour water on my bruised limbs. I wept. I then moved slowly up the back stairs of the house and made my way to the kitchen table where my small portion of curry and rice was left waiting for me.

I was starving, but I could not eat. All I could think about was my mother. Where was she? Why wasn't she here? I felt so empty inside, so deprived of my brother, my daddy, and, of course, my mom.

Oh, how I missed them!

9:00 PM - I can finally lay my head down on the hard, lumpy pillow. But wait! First I must get some coconut oil to rub my great-grandmother's feet.

Yes, I forgot to mention that my great grandmother was alive and she too lived in that small house. Rubbing the soles of her feet each night was a ritual I did not mind. She cared about me and wished me no harm and assured me that someday, all my suffering would come to an end.

She was 78 years old, and she had neither the strength nor the power to protect me. The house where we all lived still belonged to her. She told me stories of the hard work of her younger years, and how her mom was born during their ocean passage from India to Guyana. There was a lot more too.

It was time to close my eyes and hope for some sleep. I closed my eyes on another full day of hard labor and rape.

"Good night, Veemala. Try to get some rest."

That was my great-grandmother trying to comfort me, ignorant of my trials but possessing the wisdom and love to comfort me nonetheless.

CHAPTER 11

Therapist - Second Visit

THE TRAIN RIDE FROM JAMAICA, Queens to downtown Manhattan is always an adventure for me. It allows me to sit back and observe the constant movement of people, people of all nationalities and cultures.

New York, the greatest melting pot in the world.

I analyze everyone that passes by, everyone standing there before me. As they turn to disembark, I wonder if *anyone* shared the same issues and miseries I had borne.

I tried to read their thoughts and envisioned how they handled their mishaps. You see many different faces in New York; sometimes the same, sometimes new ones. Everyone looks different, and you can tell most are in their own world while *en route.*

I truly admire every face I see, everyone's skin color, shape, and size. Somehow it all makes me feel connected and relevant. I feel relaxed on the train. I have no worries. I can take one breath at a time.

My turn to step off the train. I arrive at West 4th Street at 3:39 PM. My appointment with Dr. Irene is in six minutes. I hope I am not late.

It makes me anxious. I still have four long blocks to walk. As soon I step off the train I see the hustle and bustle in the street packed with people going to and fro.

Unlike Guyana, jobs are easier to find here, and it is easier to learn a trade. My life had turned into The Great American Dream...well, sort of...

"Hi, Veemala. Dr. Irene asked that I show you to her waiting room. She apologizes for running a bit late. An emergency visit to another client," the receptionist explained to me.

Whew!. I was so relieved. Then I saw a hulking mass of a man, another patient emerging from the other doctor's office. He looked exactly like one of my attackers. I started to get scared and shake but managed to convince that this was a different time and place and I could safely wait for Dr. Irene.

"I think I'll just sit in the same comfortable chair I sat in last time," I said.

There were coffee brewing and a teapot full of hot water. Next to it was a box containing a colorful assortment of teas.

"Help yourself," said the receptionist.

After fixing myself a cup of herbal tea, I chose what is now my favorite reclining chair. As my eyes roamed around the room I tried to find Dr. Irene's personality in the furnishings, in some of the paintings on the walls. I wanted to know how her journey into psychology began. I wondered what her success rate was with people like me.

I wondered if she could actually help me make the journey back from hell,

Through the drawn drapery, I could see the darkening sky. The clouds were settled into each other, creating a dark dense shadow.

My body slid deeper into the embrace of the reclining chair.

CHAPTER 12

Deja Vu

MY MEMORY IS RUSHING BACKWARD. It is a Sunday afternoon in May 1993, when I was 15 years old. Just like today, it started with bright sunshine and cool wind as the preacher's words of hope and wisdom lingered in my head.

I had just attended a church service and made my way home where I now resided with my father, clueless as to what awaited me there.

Suddenly, the clouds darkened with the sound of thunder. Flashes of lighting lit up the sky.

I hastened home, hoping to avoid the imminent deluge of rain. Somewhere in my head I kept hearing the words: "It takes more courage to reveal insecurities than to hide them, more strength to relate to people than to dominate them, more manhood to abide by thought out principles than by blind reflex."

That was a quote from my pastor, or did I read it in some book? I wasn't sure, but it lifted my spirits and gave me some hope.

I moved to my father's house when the abuse and torture I suffered in grandmother's town became too much to bear.

We had not heard from my mother. The only other option was returning to my father.

I was back in the very same prison as before.

Inside the house, daddy was in a state of intoxicated recklessness. One day as I stepped through the door, I was literally ambushed. My father came at me with an onslaught of vicious slaps and punches. Nothing had changed. The beating would not stop until we all got away.

He lifted me up in the air, and viciously slammed me to the ground. My vision fragmented into a kaleidoscope of colors from the vibrating pain in my body. I lay there helpless, listening to the worst denigrating insults spewing from his mouth.

My father considered me worthless, inept, a scourge to the family, and deliberately dysfunctional. Life had become so unbearable at my grandmother's that I had returned to my father. This is what I came home to.

His painful words paralyzed and choked me, stopping my breath. I had grown accustomed to most of the curses and insults, but today, we reached a new depth when my father said, "SOMETIMES I WISH THAT YOU WERE NEVER BORN."

The worst thing a parent could ever say. His words rang in my ears, adding new agony, a new scar to my transfixed heart.

My life was a mess and clearly needed fixing. I wondered if any other child's life had been as shattered as mine. My head was spinning. I tottered on the brink of a bottomless chasm. Where was the remorse in my life?

I imagined I had not suffered as greatly as my mother, yet we faced the very same demon. These were wounds that would fester for the rest of my life. Entire days spent trying to suppress - to erase - my feelings, which is an impossible task. In spite of his drinking and abuse, he always made sure that my brother and I had dinner. But his words, whether from anger or ignorance, kept spinning in my head. I wasn't needed in this world anymore. Why was I still here? Why was I fighting to live, and for whom? What was the purpose of it all, anyway?

CHAPTER 13

Death As Sanctuary

YOU CANNOT STOP THE RUSH of pain as it wells up from deep inside, inflicted by someone - my father - who would just as soon see me dead.

I started to believe this would be preferable - that it would be better if I weren't here at all. If I could just vanish. Once I was gone, my family would no longer have to deal with me or who I was.

From the beginning, they all knew what was wrong with me. What didn't I understand?

The physical, emotional, psychological, and mental pain I experienced from this latest beating at the hands of my father left me broken and numb.

The pain was still there, but I could no longer feel it. Knowing that my father wished that I had never been born destroyed my soul. I needed to rest, rest, rest forever in unending sleep.

As I sat outside beneath the mango tree in the backyard of his home, my thoughts ceased. I was unable to make plans, figure out what to do or where to go next. Death was welcoming to me. Maybe I would find sanctuary there. I no longer cared if I lived or died.

I reached for the three bottles sitting in the corner of the small, makeshift shed.

I had often thought of suicide but could never find the strength or willpower to go through with it. I thought of burning myself while at my grandmother's house, but I held back because I thought things would improve sooner or later.

Now it was time.

CHAPTER 14

And On The Fourth Day...

BLACKOUT, LOST TIME - THE four days I spent not knowing - of ceasing to exist.

Somehow, I am still alive.

I was in that hospital for four days following my suicide attempt, but still not dead.

This had to be a sign.

I had to find a way to help others, had to search for the flickering precious spirit that remained lit despite my tormented life. I had been put on Earth for a reason. The challenge was to discover what that reason was.

I was discharged from the Georgetown hospital in Guyana after a week. I returned back home to my father, stepmother, and brother.

Everyone in the village knew about my suicide attempt. Understandably, I was not keen on leaving the house. My villagers christened me with a new name, Grammaxone, the weed killer (poison), that I drank along with kerosene oil and detergent to try to end my life.

I heard someone talking. It sounded like Dr. Irene.

"Nurse, how long has she been waiting?"

"Almost forty-five minutes."

"I totally forgot about her. Please, can you wake her and try to reschedule?"

On my way home, I felt extremely drained, as if I had actually gone through a therapy session. A tub of rum raisin ice cream, two slabs of chocolate, and some Indian stringy chips topped off my day.

CHAPTER 15

Holy Intervention

IT WAS A BRIGHT, SUNNY Sunday in November 1993, the same year I consumed poison and attempted suicide.

Despite feeling very good, going to church gave me hope. It was a much needed respite from the constant fear - fear of torture and physical abuse.

I am Hindu by birth, but I felt more comfortable in the Christian church where I felt welcome and less judged. It is 9:45 that morning, so I would get to the choir and sing and hear the sermon on time. My walk to church takes only five to seven minutes.

I was about fifty yards from the church when I saw three men rushing out of the liquor shop across the street.

I ran as fast as my slender legs would carry me. Not fast enough to escape the unprovoked attack by the three men. Soon I felt the beer drenching my head and shoulders, followed by the outrageous sensation of my clothes being pulled off.

Simply because I am just me…and what is "wrong" with me?

These men lived in my village and belonged to some of the groups that verbally abused me with obscenities, threats, and invective. They were my tormentors; jailers that roamed the streets of my neighborhood.

Their greatest thrill in life was to plague me.

I tried to escape, to reach my destination - the church - but it was futile. I could not fight back since they were stronger, heavier, and taller than me. To fight or defend myself was not in my DNA.

I am not a coward, not timid, but I could only fear and cower from the harsh and ugly attacks.

Instead, I always silently pray for kindness and for the strength to survive the attacks.

My prayers must have been heard. Some church attendees came to my aid. They heard and saw the assault on me and, good Christians that they were, they rushed to my defense. My drunken attackers withdrew, sauntering back like worms to the liquor store. Incidents like these caused me always to stay indoors to prevent further humiliation and attacks.

CHAPTER 16

Beach Beautiful And Deadly

It is 1994. I am almost 16 years old.

The sun was blazing and a great day for an outing on the beach. My father, stepmother, and a few other relatives from father's side of the family embarked on a four hour trip to the beach, 63 Beach, in the Cinderella county of Berbice.

Guyana is divided into three main counties: Essequibo, Demerara, and Berbice. Guyana is known as "the land with many waters" and has the largest single drop waterfall, The Kaieteur Falls, botanical gardens, and a national zoo near Georgetown.

The Kaieteur Falls are part of the Kaieteur National Park, once nominated a World Heritage Site. Guyana's wild forests are home to some of the most diversified animal and plants in the world.

On our long ride there, I could feel the tension and psychological distance from my relatives.

I was an outcast.

They were a clique, sharing inside jokes while laughing at me. This added fuel to my father's ire, giving him further license to degrade me and to blame me for anything that he deemed shameful, annoying, or uncomfortable. It was always my fault.

I never knew why, but it was.

CHAPTER 17

Ocean Tears

I DID NOT NEED MY relatives to tell me that I didn't belong there.

The negative energy and the distance I felt from them were major hints. It was obvious. I was the source of their eternal embarrassment.

I knew what was coming. I was always quiet and shy, but somehow even that drew negative attention and persecution toward me.

I slowly allowed myself to drift away from the group. I walked to a quiet spot on the sand and sat down to reflect. I had been a loner since birth, so the cold shoulder treatment situation was nothing new. I needed to relax. I found a moment of sorely needed bliss, still longing for my mother to return, for a miraculous change in my life...how long and when?

The sun was warm, and the wind was soft and cool on my skin. I could have sat there forever and been content. This seemed to be better than any other place for my wounded soul. I could release things that I could not let go of before.

I knew my healing was not permanent or complete, but I hoped for some shift from past damaging thoughts.

I watched the waves rush in and clash against the rocks, slowly rolling over themselves again to regroup and start all over again. The feeling was euphoric, but I knew it was all about to change. Any hint of hope or happiness in my life was always short-lived, disrupted by pain, sadness, and disappointment.

I felt it, cold hard liquor drenching my head as cigarette butts and seashells pelted me like hail. My ears rattled, recoiling from the vile expletives hurled my way. First I was dragged and then hurled into the air like some dirty, deflated beach ball.

I had given up on life yet I was still walking, breathing, even talking upon the Earth. I was stuck, caught between places that meant unpleasantness and harm.

Fear blinds me. This is what happens when my mind and brain shut down. Thoughts and prayers became useless ghosts and delusions as I felt the hands of several men and women on my body, dragging me towards the ocean and into the deep water. They were trying to drown me.

I sensed the approach of death, so I fought, fought to survive. With all my remaining strength, I struggled against their bodies, pushing myself up and away from their grasp.

I desperately needed air. I had to breathe. I felt strong hands around my neck, strangling me, forcing me back down. I knew this nightmare. I had to fight one more hard fight to awaken from horror.

Arms flailing, with my last ounce of strength, I made contact with someone, a woman, and I held on for dear life.

I was saved.

The men and two women released me from their grip and walked away.

I was still clinging to the woman who had saved me. She thought the whole thing was a joke. She thought we were all friends playing a silly game - water sports - so she did not intervene. Not until I held onto her arm without letting go.

Hurriedly, I made my way back to where my father sat, doing my best to appear sane. I didn't want anyone to know about the attack. No one would believe me. Worse still, they would blame me for provoking it. I could imagine my father apologizing to my assailants for the disturbance I had caused.

"You actually went into the water?" my cousin asked. I solemnly nodded.

About five minutes later, the woman who saved me came and told my father and relatives about the attack. By that time, my attackers were out of sight, nowhere to be found.

My dad thanked the woman for saving me, and then told me to stay close by! I felt protected by my daddy for the first time, but my pain, my near brush with death by drowning, overcame any other feelings.

I started to think, *maybe Daddy does care about me.* He loved me in his own peculiar way.

CHAPTER 18

Flood Of Undying Memories

SATURDAY IN QUEENS NEW YORK. I have eleven appointments in the beauty salon.

Five are for haircuts, four for color, and two new clients need extra special styling for a wedding and an engagement. They also want their makeup done.

Well, I still have time for coffee and a long hot shower.

But an admirer, Bryan, keeps crossing my mind. I am not sure if should I go out with him tonight.

I *should* play hard to get, but it has been a few weeks - feels like *forever* - since I've been out.

Suppose I do decide to meet up with him. What should I wear?

Oh well, I'll think about it while I'm at the shop.

"Hello! Hello, is anybody there?"

The voice of my aunt. My *two* aunts (Julie and Jenny). They are always together and always make the same boisterous entrance.

I was working on my last client's hair and was grateful for the break in our conversation. I gave as good as I got. I replied in the same unnecessarily loud manner. We usually spoke in our colloquial Guyanese way.

It was about 7:00 PM. My phone buzzed. It was a text from Bryan confirming our date.

"Pick me up around nine, okay?" I texted back.

The plan was dinner and drinks at a Thai restaurant. Thai food is one of my favorite cuisines, especially the pineapple fried rice.

The excitement of going out to dinner must have been written all over my face. Before I could finish my text, my two aunts were all over me wanting to know everything. Who it was, where I was going, what would I wear? They were disappointed that I was not going to join them at the local Indian restaurant. The place had good food and music, and they never tired of laughing at the drunken patrons.

They were concerned and they always warned me to be careful. I said I would be fine.

"Call us when you get home," they said.

No problem. I nodded.

CHAPTER 19

Dressing For The Kill

As I LOOK BACK ON my many past relationships, I now see my missteps. There were mistakes and wrong choices, but for some reason I am unable to correct them. I seem to make them over and over again, always hoping for a different result.

I don't know why. Why do I keep doing that?

As I pulled up the zipper of my sexiest dress, purchased from *a haute couture* designer's collection, I had flashbacks of other times, of other such preparations for dates that ended in disappointment.

I remember an older, much older man. His name was Doug, and I now consider him irrelevant.

We met on a dating website. Doug is very rich, well-connected, and lives in Pennsylvania. He was originally from Italy, which was exotic, really great.

The sex was abundant. There is no other way to put it. I was hoping to live in a big, beautiful house with the worries of my victimhood behind me. I would be safe, free from the prison of my past. After all, it's every girls dream to find love and happiness.

Doug promised all this to me. Promised me the best life I could imagine. We spent nights together, and he took me to high-end restaurants and other memorable places. Money was no object. Some weekends he would come and stay almost the entire week. Then he would leave. He said he had important meetings to attend.

I loved him dearly.

But sometimes he would snap at me. Doug hid things from me. The relationship lasted nearly three years. I gave it my all and put up with much. Gradually, then finally, he was not there for me. Romeo Doug turned into abusive Doug. He began putting me down with insults, with condemnations that over time became increasingly frequent. None of my needs were being met, yet I tolerated all of his verbal denigrations.

All of my relationships had the same thing in common: abuse. I wasted almost three years on Doug. He kept on appearing and disappearing, back and forth in my life, until I found out that he was still happily married.

The buzz on my phone brought me back to reality. My date Bryan was waiting outside. I was a bit nervous as I peeked through the windows from my bedroom and watched him standing outside his car.

Wow! Nice car, I said to myself.

And how about that pink shirt?...hhhhmmm. It takes a real man to wear pink, I thought.

He looked great and smelled great, too.

"Nice dress," he said.

"Oh, thank you," I replied.

Dinner was not disappointing. I discovered that we had a friend in common, Pamela, whom he had dated. Not only that, but he was still in a relationship with her, and I was still friends with her.

We were unscrupulous. Brain was close to six feet tall, brown in complexion and was a citizen here through naturalization from Guyana. They say "read my lips" but I say " read my eyes". It was that kind of evening.

That night Bryan and I ended up at his place, but not before we made one final stop.

He introduced me to the hookah after he offered me a drink. Afterward, we went back to his apartment. He had forgotten his driver's license, which he would need to drive me home. I knew it was a lie, but I went along with it anyway. Bryan was definitely not boring, and he kept me rapt in intelligent conversation.

I always admire a wise, smart man.

I liked the hookah. It felt good. It tasted good too. Watermelon flavor, he told me. I was completely relaxed and remember almost every moment of that night. I couldn't reject his advances, even if I wanted to.

This was a man had who begged to take me out three years ago. Now I welcomed my chance.

We had sex in every possible position, more times than I could count. The passionate kisses, the caresses, the warm, gentle touches and tender bites of an expert lover. All over my body. I love to be in control, so I rode on top, blindfolding him with my underwear and handcuffing him with my bra while wearing my red, five-inch stilettos heels.

It only made him beg for more, even after I dripped the hot melted candle wax all over his stomach and worked our way in the steaming shower with honey followed by the bare touches of ice cubes dripping downwards while licking every melted drop.

He loved it.

Here I thought I was *soooo* shy. After all I'm a Scorpio, born in the month of November.

That night, after the exhausting work out at his place, he brought me home, and we continued the steamy love session for hours until we were both totally spent from exhaustion. It was very late in the early morning when he left.

Lying naked in bed after Bryan left, I began reviewing all my past and present encounters. This was not unusual for me. These trysts and liaisons formed my life.

But as I lay there, I felt strange, just like the night before. Minutes after smoking the hookah with Bryan my body felt out of control.

Why I was unable to stop what was happening to me? Why did I lose control of my body?

My God! He had drugged me.

I was sure. At the dinner table, he asked if I ever smoked weed. I remember telling him I said no to drugs.

When I confronted Bryan about it over the phone. He just laughed, then asked if I would like to smoke some weed.

That was the end of that relationship.

Even though every other experience with him was consensual, I still could not fathom why he did what he did. I had started to like him, too.

I lay back down on my pillow and let my mind drift way back to 1996, back to the old country - Guyana.

CHAPTER 20

Recollections

I WAS NOW ALMOST 18 years old. It had been years since my mother left Guyana for Venezuela to pursue a better life. A better life for *us*. We had no idea where she was and could not understand why she had not reached out to us all those years.

There were talks of her death, talk which seriously disturbed me. I had many sleepless nights worrying about her.

Everyday survival, such as going out to the street to attend to errands or to work, only made my insomnia worse. My harassers were merciless with me, and my fear of men was wreaking havoc on my nerves.

1996 was a mixed year for me.

Easter and kite flying meant sadness. I had already (once again) left my father's house and had moved in with my next-door neighbor.

Who would want to move from their own parents at such an early age? The neighbors were kind. I had spent so much time in their home, cooking and cleaning for them, that they asked me to move in.

They knew of the severe abuse I had suffered at the hands of my father and stepmother. I guess they felt sorry for me.

The fact that I was an excellent cook (and still am!) didn't hurt. They accepted me into their home.

Blessed relief from the stress at home! I enjoyed the time we shared despite the short supply of downtime. Shakeela, her sister Fazeela, and I were all about the same age. We got along well.

I was released from my father's imprisonment.

Staying there, in the neighbors' house, was no bed of roses. There were insults and verbal abuse, mostly from the younger brother. However, they did their best to keep him from hurting me. Unlike his sisters, he was a tyrant.

The two sisters and I went to the park to celebrate Easter by flying a kite.

That did not end well.

I was attacked by several men whose kite had gotten tangled up in ours. They cursed at me and pushed me to the ground. One of them tried to rip my ear off with something that felt very sharp.

I was bleeding profusely as we were chased out of the park. I was the main target, not my friends, but me. I seemed to bring darkness on a shiny day.

Should I have locked myself away and let life pass me by?

A dark cloud hovered over me from the minute I was born. Happiness was not for me.

Was I cursed?

Maybe that's what it was: I was *cursed*. How else to explain the continuous unraveling of my life, making sense of the experiences thrust upon me? I had no parents and if anyone was going to love me, it had to be me.

It didn't matter whose house I was in. I was still imprisoned, caged, and marked with a scarlet letter for all the world to see. Despite my best intentions (I always tried to fit in), somehow, I always drew further attacks and violence toward me.

CHAPTER 21

Circle Of Life

CHRISTMAS AND BIRTHDAYS FOR MY brother and I were celebrated through the eyes of other children.

We did not see what most saw. We did not wake up to beautifully wrapped gifts under a tree. Year-round we lacked for clothes and toys. We did not go to big places or restaurants. These things were just not part of our lives.

As you can see, we were poor. The poor do not have much. The rural area we lived in was the middle of nowhere, a hole in the wall.

Those sweet things that most children received were missing from our lives. Our parents had to make do with the little they had. The children got the punches and blows that often came with impoverished, broken homes. Despite this, we were content. We dreamed that one day we too would enjoy such bountiful love.

Most children in American are brought up on Santa Claus - the big, fancy Christmas tree and some jolly bearded man coming down a hole he can barely fit through. It was different for us. Our clothing was tattered, our feet were bare, filthy from the dirt, and food scraps were scattered about.

Today, I am filled with shame as I recall the many times my brother and I had to steal small amounts of cash from relatives and friends. We had no choice. It was either that or starve.

Money brought happiness to our bellies. Being hungry is a sin, we say, but so is stealing. I still pray to God to forgive my transgressions.

Being young and essentially parentless added to our naivete and misguided behavior. Many memories pop up, obscuring the better things I have going on in my life right now. I literally have to force - and pray - my way through them.

CHAPTER 22

Finally! One Good Christmas

It was December 23, 1996, one month after my 18th birthday. Birthdays were just another regular day for me. I never was able to have a birthday party.

In walked my mother.

A mother is incomparable to anyone else on the planet. They give us life, and the Great Mother receives us during death.

A mother can be defined as a nurturer, protector, and provider to say the least. The greatest source of love, comfort, and identity.

Euphoric? I was way beyond euphoric. My heart raced, stood still, then raced some more. The palms of my hands were hot and sweaty.

I remembered how to smile. Yes, SMILE, with uncontrollable tears of joy.

To see my mother's face, to feel her arms around me, to know she was still alive; nothing mattered more.

The one who had given breath to me stood there before me.

Thank you, God. The joy of that moment replaced all the bad memories that came before.

A man and a child accompanied my mother. She had started her own family. She looked well and healthy. Nothing mattered more.

Her years of fighting dad, surviving dad, is what kept her strong.

She said she had been hospitalized for months, following a fire in the pizza restaurant at which she worked in Venezuela. She had sustained burns over 50% of her body. There was more. She had undergone surgery to remove a brain tumor.

She had been unable to contact us, she said. I couldn't process it all, but all that mattered was that *she was home.*

How come her new man had not tried to contact us, not tried to let us know what was going on? And now she had a child, my stepbrother. Questions and doubts raced through my mind. With all that recovery time, why hadn't she contacted us, her nearly parentless children?

I had no answers. All I knew was that a mother's love was priceless. That is all I could focus on. I felt my stress melt away in seconds. Although my fears and uncertainty remained, being close to my mother made life worth living again.

The man in my mother's life stayed several weeks before returning to Venezuela. He too was Guyanese. He was a dentist who lived and worked in Venezuela.

He was married and had his own set of children.

My mom suffered a lot, endured great hardship from this man. I suspected as much, even before she shared anything about this with us. But we had our mother back. She met him after she was burned and lost everything. He took advantage of her highly dependent state and literally locked her indoors to prevent her from ever contacting the outside world.

There was another child, a sister.

After arriving in Venezuela, my mother gave birth to my little sister. I had no idea that she was pregnant when she left.

Her story of a pregnant mother leaving her home to work as a housekeeper in a foreign country grew deeper and darker.

Immediately after she gave birth, my grandmother flew to Venezuela and returned with the child (my sister), who was then placed with one of my mother's sisters in Guyana. We had minimal contact with my aunt, who claimed that the little girl was her own, another complicated situation.

Soon after my mother arrived in Guyana, I rented a house for the four of us (myself, my brothers and my mother).

Times were harder than ever for me. I took care of all the bills, but I did not mind. All I wanted was to be with my little family. Being alone had gotten old, and the presence of the others gave me a feeling of comfort and safety. All I ever dreamed of was my family.

My new stepbrother was a year old, and a bit spoiled, but he was so cute, so adorable, that we all loved him. I babysat when mother had to attend some family gathering, go to market, or had other errands to do.

I enjoyed these moments; lovely moments to be inscribed in my book of thoughts.

To this day, I can't fully explain the way I treated my baby brother.

The events of my childhood must have brought out my rougher side. There were times, times that I became angry when my tougher side emerged and showed through.

There was no reason to beat my one-year-old brother. I just did. I would beat him when he smiled, when he cried, or if he got too close to me.

I would just beat him, mercilessly.

After beating him, I would take him in my arms and hug him tightly, crying and saying how sorry I was. My outbursts were unpredictable, irrational, erratic. That is what you are thinking, and no doubt you are right.

Judge me if you will. Lord knows I am not beyond reproach. I feel deep sorrow every time I think of how I treated him. I still don't understand. Beatings were a regular feature of my childhood. Maybe I thought it was the right way to act. I didn't yet know how to love.

Maybe, maybe not. I needed therapy. Possibly a psychiatrist could help more.

Revealing all this is quite embarrassing, but this is my story. No one is perfect, least of all me.

I like dreaming. Dreaming gives me hope and brings me closer to what could be.

CHAPTER 23

Unrequited Love

I WOKE WITH A TERRIBLE headache, compounded by the fact that I had an appointment with my therapist in a couple of hours.

I took my college finals yesterday. I am beyond relieved. I never imagined that going into the medical field as a surgical technologist would be so difficult.

I had lots of help but memorizing all that medical and surgical information was no small matter: I might as well have become a full-fledged surgeon instead of assisting one.

I feel a sense of pride, of accomplishment, considering where I have been and what I have experienced. Working in an operating room where I get to assist with surgeries is my single greatest achievement. Did I mention that I had a real estate sales license as well?

Succeeding at this would mean less time in the hair salon. Not a problem. I already had a booth rented out. I needed two more people to rent out the rest.

Sleep is taking me over.

I see him now as if it was yesterday. Handsome, chiseled, with a strong jaw, thick hair and a very smooth complexion. His name was Ravish.

Ravish was my first love, a love that came from the depths of my heart. A love that was neither forced nor demanded of me.

Ravish worked in the National Insurance accounting department in Guyana. He lived 20 minutes away from me, and I met him was by chance.

We bumped into each other at the movie theatre in Georgetown. On my day off, I went to see a movie. Just to spend some time alone, or so I thought!

We slammed into each other as I walked from the restroom. He was headed in the same direction. He followed me and took the seat right next to mine.

I remember the name of the movie: *Night Eyes 3*. It was an erotic film. One thing led to another and Ravish and I started flirting. He told me I was beautiful; that he was very attracted to me. I found myself nervous, shaking, and sweating.

From the very first, we had an unspoken agreement: we would keep our relationship a secret. Still, I wanted to tell the whole world! But this was my first love relationship ever, and I was not about to spoil it by spreading the news. Besides, whom would I tell? I had no confidantes.

Our secret rendezvous took place three times a week in his small room. We had to be careful. I could not get enough of him, and he felt the same way about me, but our love and our lovemaking was forbidden. Whenever I missed him, (which was all the time) I would call him at work, and he loved it. It kept us both stimulated and excited.

One month of this and then it abruptly ended.

Ravish avoided me at every turn. My phone calls went mostly unanswered. When it was answered, it was someone else he had asked to take the call. He wanted to get rid of me.

I spent many sleepless nights thinking about Ravish. Finally, I called his work, demanding to speak with him.

That was when my heart was shattered.

The girl who answered the phone took great pleasure telling me how disgusted Ravish was of me, how he never wanted to see me again. *I was not his type.* In the end, she warned me of the beating he intended for me if I kept pursuing him.

The break up with Ravish fit perfectly in the same box I kept the rest of the torture, rapes, beatings, and degradations I had endured. It was 1:30 when I awoke from this disturbing dream of my past love. Once again I had missed my appointment with Dr. Irene, but I needed sleep.

CHAPTER 24

Sunrise And Sunset

THE PASSING OF MY FATHER left me drained of any emotion.

February 12, 2001: the date of my father's death. He was hospitalized for about a month, diagnosed with kidney failure.

Years of alcohol abuse contributed to his kidney disease. I was worried about my father. I wanted him to live to a ripe old age; perhaps we would have been able to talk about his mistreatment of me. I felt guilty, too. I could not take care of him, as most other children do with their older folks.

He left us that day, far sooner than I expected. The next day we made the funeral arrangements. I took care of every expense. I felt like I did my share. Despite all the hurt, abuse, and neglect my father doled out, I could never have ill will towards him because I know he loved me.

I took some solace in the fact that he found a small measure of peace in his final days. I wish I could have shared in that peace.

Living in our impoverished third world country and having only the most minimal education contributed to his ignorance. But he loved me, and I loved him back. Those are the facts. I ask God each day to allow me a forgiving heart and unending love for all, including my enemies.

I pray for his soul and ask God to grant him forgiveness. Even now, as I write this, I wish he was alive. I wish he could have come to America and experience freedom and civilization.

He was born and raised in an ignorant society and practiced ignorance until the day he died. If he were alive today, he would have been able to travel out of that ignorant society and experience modern life with all the love the world has to offer. Maybe he would have enjoyed having his children at his side. Unfortunately, he did not live to see that day. I still remember when I was very little, my daddy used to buy me ice cream whenever he had extra money. There are days that I still cry. I sometimes cried when I wished he was here. As we got closer before he passed away, I understand why he was ignorant and violent towards me. He thought by doing what he did was going to change me to his expectations, but that still wasn't the way to act towards a child.

CHAPTER 25

___

Walking Through The Valley Of The Shadow Of Death

AT AGE 23 YEARS, I was managing a video shop. The work was not especially hard.

I loved what I did, but people, things, and sometimes the place itself works against one's peace of mind and ability to succeed.

Running a business is not all fun and games! You have to invest much time and effort into creating a successful workplace. There were good days, and there were bad days. Some nights were overwhelming.

Running your own business takes determination, and though an income is not guaranteed the way it is in a 9 to 5 job, the freedom of being your own boss is well worth the wait.

I had taken off a week for my father's funeral. This was my first day back. For some reason, I just didn't feel like being here. Uneasy and restless, I kept looking towards at the clock, hoping that closing time would come. Closing time is nine each night and, as usual, as that time approached, I

___

always got tense and nervous, considering the neighborhood the store was located in.

Georgetown was so different from New York City, yet its shadow seemed to follow me wherever I went.

No matter that New York was affluent. Thoughts of being attacked or of being "found out" still troubled me.

Probably my mind was playing tricks on me.

I was no longer trapped in violent, hostile Guyana. Being here in New York is awesome. America is the land of opportunity and the food basket of the world.

This perspective helped me maintain a good steady mindset that crazy New York streets were far better than the streets at home.

At the stroke of nine that night, I locked the door and proceeded to count the cash in the register. Usually this takes 20 to 30 minutes.

Locking the doors of the store behind me, I hurried down the street towards the bus stop. It is was about a five-minute walk, but the entire area seemed particularly dark and dangerous that night.

Five yards from the bus stop, I approached two big, shadowy trees on the right side of the street. There I was bum-rushed by at least six men, who knocked me down and dragged me from the road to the dark edge of the sidewalk under the tree.

Just like old times. Tragedy followed tragedy, as though I was put upon this earth to receive hurt and pain. My head was spinning, my mind was racing, and my throat was dry. Unbearable misery and speechlessness visited me again.

The assailants' angry words were very confusing. They were accusing me of voting for and taking part in the opposition party's propaganda in the recent election.

All of this was untrue, absolutely senseless. Just a flimsy excuse to attack me.

Suddenly, I saw the shiny blade of a knife. The next moment, its cold, hard metal pressed hard at the bottom of my eye.

"I am going to dig out your eyes with this knife," said the man. "And then we're going to take turns raping you...and ripping your apart."

One of the others chimed in, "We will cut you open and do whatever we want with you."

Did they think about what they were doing? Would they attack their mothers this way? Or were they cold, conscienceless, not caring about - or even enjoying -terrorizing others?

My belief in the goodness and kindness of others was unreal, a treasured illusion that dissolved away.

I heard my screams in my head, but they could not come out of my mouth. I felt pieces of me being torn like it was nothing.

I was nothing.

Scary untangled threads of similar moments in my life flashed through my mind. Nothing but shame and guilt had entered my heart from the second this all started.

Who would save me?

I kept hope alive; maybe I could be saved. I felt the bile in my stomach float to my throat, threatening to suffocate me, and still I was unable to scream. Fear has paralyzed my throat along with my entire body.

Suddenly, I felt pain. My hair being chopped from my head with a knife by a different assailant. Next my pants were viciously ripped from my lower body.

I always wear leggings under my jeans, a precaution born of the countless times I had been attacked and molested and viciously raped. My only defense was to wear as many undergarments as possible.

That was the only way I knew to fight back.

Then I felt a sharp pain in my shoulder as my undergarments were cut away.

The sound of a vehicle, the focused glare of bright lights on us, saved my life. I felt the many hands of my attackers release me, and they ran from fear of being caught. I could hear them shouting at me, "If you tell the police we will hunt you down and kill you in 24 hours." They yelled the very same words as the others who had harmed me in my life.

I wish the strength I have now, I had back then. The driver of the car took me to the Georgetown Public Hospital where I was treated with stitches on my elbow and two other parts on my body.

I then lied to my mother when I got home. I told her that I had a fall at work while trying to stock the shelves with video cassettes and DVDs. Regardless of how one judged her, my mother always worried about us. Mothers always know their children best. I was not what they expected - why? Just because I loved differently. My body said one thing and my heart said another.

CHAPTER 26

More Pain, Yet Hope Is Reborn

TONIGHT, I AM GOING TO watch another new premier Lifetime movie.

The movie is about the triumph of good over evil and victory over temptations and the defeat of adversaries.

I put on the television and flipped through the channels. I saw "Breaking News. Man burns woman to death."

This also impacted me. I thought about *my* past experiences with burns and men. Throughout my life, despite its ups and deep downs, I continued grasping at hope, recalling that the sun rose every day, vanquishing the night. I could not allow any more rain to drown my parade. Life had already thrown too many sticks and stones my way. I was excited about the up and coming holiday.

Our traditional and festive National Republic Day dispelled my gloom.

Many in our country took this day seriously. The celebration gave renewed hope to the community. The holiday was comparable to the Fourth of July in the U.S.A.

When it comes to holidays, we go above and beyond. The festivities and spectacle make for one of the brightest points of the year.

This is the anniversary of the date when Guyana became a republic, and it signifies freedom from slavery. You will see crazy outbursts, people who look like they have been in hiding, waiting for this day to arrive.

Guyana celebrates *Mashramani* every year on February 23. The day marked our continuing fight for freedom from slavery begun in 1763. This is well known as the Slavery Rebellion.

The fight against slavery continued, with another revolt in 1823, the Demerara Rebellion. As many as 13,000 slaves rose up against their oppressors. The rebels were crushed, but their righteous cause continued. By 1838, total emancipation was achieved.

Our ancestors rebelled, fighting to protect their region and their rights, and they won. This movement caused many Europeans to flee; only half of them remained.

Despite the abolition of slavery, Guyana remained under British rule until the 19th century. Then, on May 26th, 1966, it became an independent country. During the time of celebration, all of the country gathers and rejoices with dancing, music, and performing artists. Parades pass through the street, featuring large floats that take days and weeks to construct. All types of people are on the streets, waving Guyana flags and dressed in ethnic attire. Imagine thousands of humans gathered for one big party, a one day carnival.

You can barely see over your shoulder. The only way to be heard is by yelling. The parade is a beautiful sight, a living commemoration and memorial to what our brave ancestors endured.

My co-worker, Bibi, invited me out to the grounds to enjoy the day. This was much needed downtime, so I agreed to go. What harm could it do?

She reassured me that she would watch over me like a hawk. I had no intention of getting very involved. I just wanted to step back and watch from the sidelines. I trusted Bibi. Our relationship had grown tighter.

Ever since we started working together, I assumed that I could accept her in my life. Life is all about change, constant change, so I had to eventually deal with not seeing her that much.

I was happy when Bibi and I worked the same shift. She had a laugh that could wake an entire neighborhood; it might even break glass. It was good having her around to support me, to be there for me.

I longed for that kind of friendship and our time together at the parade. I was able to relax for a while. We enjoyed ourselves, enjoyed all the extravagant and beautiful moments as day became night.

We decided to leave before it got too late. It was getting dark. The parade goers were still walking around the streets filled with cheer. Pushing our way through a thick mass of shoulders and dancing revelers we encountered a group of guys.

I had not particularly noticed them, but they had noticed us. They reminded me of a pack of lions waiting to devour a piece of raw meat in the wild. They were sitting outside a bar near the parade route, barbecuing their chicken on a grill.

I remember the scene like it happened yesterday.

The bar was on Vissengen Road in Georgetown, right along the way to Bibi's car. It was like some Discovery Channel travelogue, showing the lions sniffing the air as they got closer and closer, ready to attack.

They hollered at us from across the street and trying their vociferous best to get our attention. We were trying to reach home, chalking it off as a good day.

As they came into view, my friend Bibi began to cry for help. Things quickly escalated. Maybe these guys had seen me before, perhaps at the video club I recently worked.

Things just got worse. These guys were not just after Bibi, but they were going for me as well. I screamed out as they attacked me, hearing their horrible voices, their descriptions of how they would hurt me. Crazy that the day had gone so well, only to turn into another nightmare.

I had felt an aching pain in my heart from the combined humiliation and embarrassment. Dealing with this, not to mention the crowds of people that stood around, was degrading in the extreme. I mean, getting trapped in such a situation while everyone else milled at a safe distance - another shameful moment.

"I'm not who you think I am! I'm not what you think I am!" I screamed out, trying to get them to back off. Screaming out didn't help one bit.

You would think the others around would intervene, would somehow try to stop the situation, but no one came to save us. I was speechless now, profoundly ashamed, being dragged across the street like that in full view of the others.

They pulled me closer to their grill, dragging me towards the fire. Brutally, I was forced closer to the hot coals until my shoulders and stomach were burned. One of the assailants wielded a stick of burning wood. Bibi reached for me, barely saving me in time.

She caught me before they could burn my face. Running, we reached Bibi's place and caught our breath, now that we were safe. I hid everything that happened from my mother, not wanting to burden her any further with my pain. It was business as usual.

The streets of my country had become as much of a prison as my father's house had been. No matter where I went, the abuse followed me, like a shadow or a faithful dog. This time it was done by strangers and not by someone I knew.

Before we reached my house, Bibi took me to the police station. She insisted. As we went, the police suggested that all this had to stop. That I should change my voice, my clothes, my lifestyle, and not be the person I really was.

Become a normal person and stop inviting this misery upon myself would end all these troubles.

Little did they know, I always tried. I tried so hard to fit in, to conform, but somehow I seemed to be inviting more tragic moments into my life. The moments of encountering humiliation and threats were innumerable. I endured the same kind of attacks at the video store.

At times I had been abused and accused by Guyanese attackers - no surprise - who threatened to kill me. They justified their violence by assuming that I had voted for the Indian President.

Guyana has a history of false political allegations, many of them quite crazy. I was ridiculed at work simply because of my appearance. Even though PNC (the opposition party) was right upstairs from where I worked, I didn't get many threats from them. They just stared as they stood at the entrance.

One incident followed another, but the parade was a welcome break from these, while it lasted. In this world, we must choose wisely, so that we do not add to the pain that the world always seems to offer.

CHAPTER 27

Farewell

I SAID MY GOODBYES AND left Guyana in late 2002, hoping to find work in Brazil.

I planned for all to go well and hoped to be able to work my way to the top. I could not get a job the week I was there and had to figure out what I would do next. It was dreadful. I had to accept the fact that I could not find work and once again packed my bags for Guyana.

Flying on an airplane for the first time was exciting, a truly great experience. I felt like I was flying away from everything and everyone, away from pain. But I was wrong.

Totally wrong.

Days went by, and I found myself in an internet café chat room, which kindled a flame inside me. Here I met, via the internet, a guy named Prince.

It sounds unrealistic to think you and another person online could build a future together, huh? Growing up, I knew nothing about the internet or any related technology. This stuff was all new to me, but I always enjoyed learning and expanding my horizon. (Eventually education rescued my life.) I took a crash course in computer 101. I wanted to pursue education so that I would not have to depend on anyone for anything.

Survival was my priority.

Today, in the U.S., I am still learning. Sometimes I feel like a newborn in an adult body.

We had our long conversations, and I found myself once again packing to leave. We would meet in the Bahamas sometime in April 2003.

My life had always been chaotic. So I thought, *how bad could this be?*

I asked my Aunt Pam, and she sent me a plane ticket to the Bahamas. (Pam lives here in the U.S., and it was her home that I went to and stayed at after release from the detention center.)

She and I grew close over time and, despite being my youngest aunt, Pam became my surrogate mother figure. I got all the financial and other support from her.

She cut my hair off the next day after I moved in! She, too, thought I could change.

Anyone searching for a replacement of love that they never had can surely relate.

My stay in the Bahamas lasted about two months.

I had graduated in Guyana as a nail technician, so there were a lot of jobs and people wanting to hire me. In order to get a job in the Bahamas, I had to leave the island, apply for a work permit, and then return to the Bahamas.

I could not have afforded it financially, and the sexual harassment three times a night from Prince was unbearable. Besides, there was no one else to turn to. Prince worked at a local gas station in the Bahamas and tried to help me, but he was struggling himself.

Once again, the emotional roller coaster was rising and falling.

The last day of my stay there, I was forced to buy my return ticket to Guyana. I had tried and failed; nothing else seemed possible anymore.

At least I knew what to expect back at home - death.

I could not go back there, to that jail. It seemed as if the entire country was against me. The land that I grew up in and called home was toxic to my very being. I knew little else but this prison. Was I destined to be chained there forever?

CHAPTER 28

Land Of Liberty

AFTER I BOUGHT MY AIRFARE and walked out of the travel agent's office, I sat in a park not far away. It was a beautiful Saturday afternoon, July 5, 2003.

In the midst of my daydreaming, I was brought back to reality when an older black woman approached me saying, "My child, why are you crying? You are so young and beautiful. Who and what can possibly be the reason for your hurt? Girl, you better wipe those tears." She was short, about 4 feet 4 inches tall, with gray hair, brown skin, and she wore a pearl white dress. Her English was fluent, and she descended upon me like a merciful angel.

I was still searching for peace. I told her my story. She shocked me. She said that regardless of what I had been through, I was still beautiful and that God is testing my faith. Prayers, music, and Lifetime movies were, and still are, my therapy.

Prayers gave me faith; yes, lots of faith. Faith in the belief that there is always a better tomorrow.

Music eased my distress, and practically every Lifetime movie made me aware that I was not alone, that I was not the only one suffering. The music and the movies gave me hope for a better life ahead. Those were the strengths I lived by. The words of that old lady still echo in my ears to this day.

"I am sorry you have been through all those horrible things, but your life is not over yet," she continued. "You are on this Earth for a big, big reason and I assure you that you will see it one day. Now, since your flight is stopping in Miami and you have to change planes, why don't you ask for political asylum?"

I never heard of any words like "political asylum" before, but all else had failed. Would asking for asylum change anything or make a difference?

The flight was short, 40 minutes in all from the Bahamas. I landed at Miami International Airport the evening of July 5th around 5:00 pm. I did not have a visitor's visa, so I could not leave the airport. In fact, when the plane landed, I was detained by an immigration officer who walked with me to a room. I was supposed to stay locked in that room for the next two hours until my flight back to Guyana was ready to board. I had just landed here in the U.S.A., the melting pot of the world, yet I was not allowed to explore or see this wonderful land.

After about an hour in custody, I told the officer that I did not want to go back to Guyana because I feared for my life, that I would like to apply for political asylum.

She looked at me like "*What?*"

"Excuse me, what did you just say?"

I told her again that my life was in danger. She called another officer, who came and tried to convince me to go back home and that if I lost in the asylum process, I would be banned from the United States for a period of ten years or more. I would not be able to visit or see my grandparents ever.

I had been refused a visitor's visa twice before, but now that I was already here, I was willing to take that chance.

"I don't care if that happens, sir, but I want to apply for asylum," I told him.

I was treated like a criminal throughout the whole process. But there was no way I was going back. I knew there was light on the other side on these shores, so I chose asylum.

I may have been put in an actual prison, but I was closer to freedom than ever before. With all the struggles and abuse I received growing up, and with all that abuse still waiting for me at home, I knew this was the only way I might have a life. A life that was free.

Later that night, I was interviewed by another officer who ruled on my stay in a detention center. He said, "You will get a chance to speak to an asylum officer. If that officer determines that you have a credible fear of returning to your country, you will then have the opportunity to speak with an immigration judge. That judge will then decide if you get to stay in the U.S.A."

The next morning, I was transferred to a detention center in Miami, Florida. Three days later, I was sent to the Elizabeth Detention Center in New Jersey.

It was the most horrible flight ever. I was chained across my legs, and the handcuffs bit at my wrists as I walked to and from and through the entire airports.

Can you imagine someone looking at you, thinking you are a criminal? That's how I felt: numb and ashamed but going with the flow. I didn't have a choice.

I remained in detention for exactly two months and three days. This was by far, one of the strangest experiences I had known. I was inside a dormitory with 40 men.

These moments were awkward, uncomfortable in the extreme. I was the closest thing to a woman they had probably seen in years. All eyes were on me from the very first day.

As attention rose, I asked to be put in protective custody inside the prison for my own safety. That was not a pretty sight. The little prison was a cold place to be put into and a hard place to lay one's head at night. I still kept hope alive. It was safer for me inside than out. One small toilet and a twin-sized bed with mattress made of papers instead of sponge, at least that is how it felt. Nothing was real, and I was very confused and scared. I worried about my health, and I wondered if I would ever get out. I thought I would go insane. Some detainees had been there over four years waiting for their case to be called or to be deported.

Writing my story - writing, writing, writing - kept me from losing my mind.

While in custody, I watched a security guard stand out front to secure my door. One day, in the month of September 2003, I was woken up by one of the guards around 4:30 AM. He told me it was time for me to leave.

There was an explanation to the seeming miracle. My grandmother retained an attorney, and finally I was let off on parole. The only condition was showing up for my court dates. So, I spent two months and three days in a detention center in New Jersey

Things were looking up!

I was eternally grateful for being able to live with my grandmother in New York City. This was the time that my Aunt Pam snipped off my hair, hoping to change me back. I had no choice but to respect her will. After all, I was going to reside in her home.

Now, many people hear the words *political asylum* but without wholly understanding what they mean.

In the United States, asylum may be given to people who are afraid to return home because of persecution on account of their race, religion, nationality, social group, or political persuasion. If you are granted asylum, you can live and work in the U.S.A. and, after one year, you can file adjustment of status to become a permanent resident.

To start the process, a person seeking asylum must be in a U.S. territory. To ask for asylum, a "USCIS" (United States Citizenship and Immigration Services) form must be filled out in its entirety. The processing is completed within 180 days of the date of filing.

This was definitely a step in the right direction. As I stayed with my grandmother at my aunt's house, I started to look around and then was hired as a nail technician. I did what you would expect - file nails and provide a great deal of customer service.

One woman spoke to me about going to beauty school. Beauty school certification is well known in New York State. There is competition for jobs in the better salons, but there still seemed to be room for me.

I took the woman's advice and encouragement, thanked her, and enrolled in a school. I learned many trades in beauty school. Soon enough, I was on my way to graduating as a cosmetologist and beautician. This was a life-changing event that would do me well.

After 18 months in beauty school, I graduated with a beauty degree in my hand. I hope the tale of my remarkable transformation motivates and inspires others who have all but given up.

No pain, no gain. You either keep hope alive or you give up.

My advice? I say, *Don't give up!* Trouble does not always last, and that is a fact. In other words, "This too shall pass." We sometimes do not get to pick and choose what comes our way, but we can always try to keep our hearts and minds prepared for what may come. I had graduated and was now working inside a local salon.

This was freedom to me.

I slowly built up my clientele and, eventually, owned my own salon. The key to my freedom was now in *my* hands. I began to be happy with my life and all that it had brought me.

I managed my finances to the point where I could afford my own apartment. I moved out from under my aunt and grandmother. It was another stepping stone to independence.

CHAPTER 29

Transformation

I HAD THIS ONE QUESTION in my mind: when would I be able to afford my surgery? It was my most pressing desire.

Sexual reassignment surgery for male-to-female involves reshaping the male genitals into a form with the appearance of, and, as far as possible, the function of female genitalia. Before any surgery, patients usually undergo hormone replacement therapy (HRT), and, depending on the age at which HRT begins, facial hair removal. There are associated surgeries patients may elect to, including facial feminization surgery, breast augmentation, and various other procedures.

When changing anatomical sex from male to female, the testicles are removed, and the skin of foreskin and penis is usually inverted, as a flap preserving blood and nerve supplies (a technique pioneered by Sir Harold Gillies in 1951), to form a fully sensitive vagina (vaginoplasty). A clitoris fully supplied with nerve endings (innervated) can be formed from part of the glans of the penis. If the patient has been circumcised (removal of the foreskin), or if the surgeon's technique uses more skin in the formation of the labia minora, the pubic hair follicles are removed from some of the scrotal tissue, which is then incorporated by the surgeon within the vagina.

Other scrotal tissue forms the labia majora. Usually this kind of surgery can last anywhere from six to eight hours.

In extreme cases of shortage of skin, or when a vaginoplasty has failed, a vaginal lining can be created from skin grafts from the thighs or hips, or a section of colon may be grafted in (colovaginoplasty).

Surgeon's requirements, procedures, and recommendations vary enormously in the days before and after, and the months following, these procedures.

Plastic surgery, since it involves skin, is never an exact procedure, and cosmetic refining to the outer vulva is sometimes required. Some surgeons prefer to do most of the crafting of the outer vulva as a second surgery, when other tissues, blood and nerve supplies have recovered from the first surgery. This is is relatively minor surgery, which is usually performed only under local anaesthetic, is called labiaplasty.

The aesthetic, sensational, and functional results of vaginoplasty vary greatly. Surgeons vary considerably in their techniques and skills, patients' skin varies in elasticity and healing ability (which is affected by age, nutrition, physical activity and smoking), any previous surgery in the area can impact results, and surgery can be complicated by problems such as infections, blood loss, or nerve damage.

Because of the risk of vaginal stenosis (the narrowing or loss of flexibility of the vagina), any current technique of vaginoplasty requires some long-term maintenance of volume (vaginal dilation), by the patient, using medical graduated dilators to keep the vagina open. Penile-vaginal penetration with a sexual partner is not an adequate method of performing dilation. Daily dilation of the vagina for six months in order to prevent stenosis is recommended among health professionals. Over time, dilation is required less often, but it may be required indefinitely in some cases.

Regular application of estrogen into the vagina, for which there are several standard products, may help, but this must be calculated into total estrogen dose. Some surgeons have techniques to ensure continued depth, but extended periods without dilation will still often result in reduced diameter (vaginal stenosis) to some degree, which would require stretching again, either gradually, or, in extreme cases, under anesthesia.

With current procedures, trans women are unable to receive ovaries or uterus. This means that they are unable to bear children or menstruate until a uterus transplant is performed, and that they will need to remain on hormone therapy after their surgery to maintain female hormonal status and features but I didn't need hormones because I already had the imbalance in my body from birth.

Here is a thumbnail sketch of the costs involved. Before the actual surgery, there were mandatory therapy sessions at $150 to $250 per session.

Letters from two or more therapists are usually needed for surgery of this kind. The total cost of therapy and the letters can range from under $1,000 to more than $5,000 per year. Hormone therapy cost an additional $300 to $2,400 per year.

$40,000 for the operation itself.

This is what people contemplating this kind of surgery go through. Myself, I was just happy about being able to finally start living my life the way I wanted to, without external constraints, although I was still living in a West Indian community in Richmond Hill, Queens.

The next step in my journey to transformation involved taking the necessary medication.

Things had definitely changed, of course, by the time my surgery took place. The strength and muscle power that got me through my chores in Guyana were gone after the surgery.

Part of me felt weaker, but there was no change in my sense of who I was. The only change I could feel was physical.

After surgery, I started to gain weight, picking up pounds as my body changed shape. Parts of my body, like the area around my hips, grew larger. I was a full-blown woman, curves and all, at this point. I was told that I had now become a woman, 100% female.

I think back on my fantasies, my daydreams as a child. They helped me get through the years of abuse, whether physical, sexual, or verbal.

Now, when I look at myself, I see my daydreams alive in the real world. A world I always wanted to live in. I am now so encouraged to live life and want to explore and learn about different things and meet different people.

As I have mentioned more than a few times, my life experiences have compelled me to help others. Before I bring my story to a close, I want to share in these next chapters, some important things I have talked about to others and groups. I did this one-on-one, in front of a group, or via my YouTube videos. I think you can see how my life has shaped my thinking and stirred my passions on these topics.

CHAPTER 30

Thoughts On Education

I BELIEVE DEEPLY IN THE importance of education and knowledge. An educated person is an empowered person— someone who is aware of the world around them and who knows which options and pathways are available. I feel strongly about education. It is both tragic and remarkable that in this day and age, millions must face the obstacle of inadequate or absent education. Education is a right, not a privilege. Food, water, shelter, health care are very important, and education is right up there, as essential to life as a sound body and mind.

My story is solid proof of this. As a child in an impoverished third world country, my education was minimal. I didn't get much beyond grade school. My schooling always took a back seat to the seemingly urgent daily chores such as tending the farm, cleaning the house, and even doing other labor. Once I came to the United States, I was overwhelmed at the many paths that suddenly opened before me. Unlike my native country, this is a country where people are empowered to follow and fulfill their dreams—by education! Although I arrived on these shores as a poor, directionless immigrant, I quickly found dozens of resources at my disposal and dozens of people and groups and agencies willing to help. Within months, I was earning a salary as a beautician and went on from there to continue and complete my education. Now I am a surgical technologist and a motivational speaker.

Education is not the only key to success, but it does show you the way to your dreams!

CHAPTER 31

Thoughts On Writing

YOU ARE READING THIS EDITION of my book. Call me resourceful, call me a self-starter, but the fact remains that once I came to this country, I seized many of the opportunities available to me, not the least of which was education. I have described my evolution as an entrepreneur and a health caregiver. I also owe my career as a writer to the people and other resources who made it possible for me to complete my education and share the roadmap of my good fortune by the powerful act of writing. The pen is mightier than the sword. The pen is also mightier than ignorance, prejudice, and an unnecessarily substandard quality of life. Teaching and learning are the DNA that helps individuals and society continue to evolve; to become more self-reliant and effective.

When I came to the USA, I finally got the chance to tell my story. I wanted to talk about my transformation from a severely depressed victim to a successful, sought after woman. My mission is to tell my story in order to help other victims of poverty, ignorance, and abuse. I want to motivate and inspire others.

The woman I am today went through hell but survived the journey. I wanted my book to tell the true story of a child raised in Guyana by a family and society intolerant of the child's way of loving. I graphically wrote about horrific episodes of rejection, physical and emotional abuse, violence, and rape. I wanted my journey from victimhood to achieving my college degree as a beautician, and now a surgical technologist. I needed to offer my message of hope to all victims of abuse, social intolerance, and marginalization. I want to give my readers hope and faith as it relates to all of life's difficult experiences.

CHAPTER 32

Thoughts On Self-Esteem

BUILDING HEALTHY SELF-ESTEEM IS A process that starts way back in infancy and childhood. Children learn early on how they feel about themselves from their interaction with their parents and other caregivers. Self-esteem is as important to health and happiness as good nutrition, sunshine, and air. The love and care that parents show children by repeated examples showing the child that she or he is highly valued, greatly appreciated, and is a gift to the world is the key.

From childhood on, many of us constantly wonder, "Am I good enough? Do people like me? Am I a worthwhile person whom others will want to know and spend time with?"

Low self-esteem—not liking yourself or your appearance, feeling that you don't fit in, that you are not as good as others—is toxic. Low self-esteem leads to so many problems in life. Many unfortunate people who doubt their value and self-worth spend their precious time on earth trying to prove they are worth more than they believe. They can even overcompensate for feelings of low self-esteem.

A person who considers him or herself a loser goes about proving his beliefs by engaging in self-destructive behavior and destructive relationships. Many people with addictions such as alcoholism and drug and sexual abuse are trying to escape feelings or self-medicated self-esteem problems. People we think of as narcissists—those for whom everything is about "me"—can be ambitious and even quite successful, but they never succeed at achieving love and intimacy with others. As the saying goes, if you can't love yourself, then how can you love someone else?

Healthy self-esteem leads to healthy and happy relationships and good self- care. Having self-esteem and achieving self-worth and self-respect provide the emotional and spiritual nutrition that make life worth living. At the end of the day when you honestly feel you've lived a meaningful, valuable, loving day, and you can jump out of bed with happy anticipation of the day ahead, you are living life to the fullest.

What's more, there is no going back. Once you've tasted the rewards of contentment, self- confidence, and the knowledge that you are trying to make the world a better place, you wouldn't have it any other way.

A quote that I once read mentioned that to eat, move, speak, and act as you love yourself is a great way of achieving high self-esteem. Every day you should look in the mirror and say to yourself, "I've been through a lot, but I am still standing here. I love me, respect me, and I am proud of me." Remember, life is not about the content but all about the context.

CHAPTER 33

Thoughts On Faith

PEOPLE OFTEN ASK ME ABOUT the role of faith in my life. Where does faith come in? I can tell you that a little faith can go a long, long way. Faith is not something you can measure with a ruler or on a scale. Nonetheless, countless people attribute their survival, well-being, and success to keeping faith.

"Long, dark nights of the soul," are those times when we don't know how we will make it to the next morning, or even the next hour. Eventually, we have to surrender to the white light of a lasting, unshakeable faith.

I would not have survived the brutal ordeals of my childhood and adolescence without some inner sense that I would eventually get through these times and find the light at the end of the tunnel. Having faith is like believing in miracles, and miracles happen all the time. Remember, faith is courage and courage is hope, so have faith.

CHAPTER 34

Thoughts On Self- Worth & Self-Respect

I LOVE MY LIFE, AND I want to make it possible for others limited by their gender at birth to achieve self-realization and expression. This also includes everyone else who might be suffering from maintaining their self-worth.

You see, when I get up in the morning, I look forward to the events of the day, even when I'm anticipating a heavy work schedule. I prepare for the day ahead, just like most other people do. Now, my appearance is very important to me, Looking good makes me feel good. Taking care of my appearance and being the best person I can be, whether at work, with friends, or at home, are incredibly important to my self-worth and self-respect.

"To each his own," they say. So it goes when it comes to self-worth and self-respect. One person may measure his or her self-worth by the size of his or her bank account or collection of designer shoes. Others base self-worth on less tangible, less materialistic qualities such as kindness and their ability to contribute to the world in a meaningful way.

The same goes for self-respect. Some people don't give a second thought to impulses and behaviors that would cause most others to recoil in fear or disgust. Self-respect may or may not be based on a clear conscience - on the feeling that one is living one's life in a loving, compassionate, and morally evolved way. Others, often referred to as sociopaths or anti-social personalities, seem to lack for reasons we don't understand the capacity for a conscience and have no problem with harming themselves or others in the pursuit of what they want.

When you feel you've done your best and given your most, you find that you may be able to rest easy at night. It's a feeling of innocence. It's a feeling that can't be beat because self-worth leads to self-respect, which then leads to self-discipline. We don't need a fancy car or a big bank account to give us those qualities. It starts by loving yourself first and preserving your pride and dignity.

CHAPTER 35

Thoughts On Self-Confidence

NOT EVERYONE CAN DEFINE WHAT self-confidence is or even have the strength and courage or faith to embrace it. Without self-confidence, you cannot get anywhere. Like they say, "You always take yourself with you!" A self-confident person is resilient, spontaneous, effective, and happy. It is someone who can walk into a new situation or a group of new acquaintances and carry him or herself with poise, dignity, and vivacity for life.

When you are certain that you are an important good person whose presence is sought after by others, you don't have to spend valuable time worrying about whether you will be accepted or rejected. There are so many more important and better things to think about! Self-confidence gives you the energy and curiosity to care deeply about the world and the people around you.

Since you are self-confident, you have plenty of energy left over for other people and pursuits in life. Each and every day, we encounter new and unfamiliar challenges. Self-confidence gives us the rocket fuel - the courage - to engage the unfamiliar or unknown with eagerness and grace. It all starts with believing in yourself, taking risks, or any experience that reveals the human spirit.

CHAPTER 36

Thoughts On Motivation

I'M OUT THERE TELLING MY story in the hope that it will motivate others to follow my example. Given the number of obstacles involved, a high level of motivation is key to succeeding at becoming yourself.

What's the difference between two people working at the same task, one of whom succeeds while the other fails? Motivation. Why is it that some people seem always to be able to get what they want out of life while the rest of us can only sit on the sidelines and look on. Same answer! Motivation is a complex personality trait almost equivalent to encouragement. Each of us is born with biologically different levels of motivation. Some of us are self-starters, while others are just passive, watching the parade go by them. High motivation is a destination with many different roads leading to it. We all know individuals who are motivated to succeed by the example of role models, including parents, teachers, and friends.

Sometimes our desire to achieve or to succeed is a matter of defining ourselves. "I am a person who succeeds." Or, "I am a person who has the will-power and self-discipline to get wherever it is I need to go." The list of motivators is practically endless. Some people are attracted to wealth, fame, or power, and these are sufficient to provide the impetus to outdo oneself and achieve one's personal best. Perhaps the most powerful motivator of all is the knowledge that we are doing our best and our hardest for the sake of another. A belief in something bigger than ourselves—in a divinity or God—is often the chief motivation for superb creative and spiritual experiences. For me, the knowledge that I am helping others is a very strong personal motivator. Remember, motivation leads to success.

CHAPTER 37

Thoughts On Power

SO MANY KINDS OF POWER! There is the power of a jet fighter soaring beyond visibility in the blink of an eye. There is the quiet elegant power of the person who can see beyond the immediate moment and refrain from reacting impulsively. Creative and spiritual power taps into unknown sources and brings out the best in us, whether we are painting a picture or meditating on a quiet beach. Power comes from knowing yourself and pacing and applying your energy in the most effective and sophisticated ways.

Too many relationships are based on power, on the domination of one partner by the other. Like water and electricity, power can be used for good or negative purposes. The relationship between parent and child, or between teacher and student are necessarily power-based, and these relationships run the gamut from kind, loving mentorships to brutal and cruel situations where one party takes advantage of the other. The more evolved we become, the greater our power.

Focusing power on helping others and on reaching higher and higher personal goals is a great skill that can in part be taught. Because many, if not most of us, learn by example, it

---

is especially important to interact with and be surrounded by people whose attitudes are positive and who have your best interest at heart. For too many years, the power axis between men and women has been skewed toward the man. This polarity is changing now, in many places and in many ways. We know that matriarchal societies have come and gone over the course of human history. We also know that women can be tough and that men can be vulnerable.

Reaching my goals and becoming the person I was meant to be has empowered me. I hope and pray to use this power wisely and in the service of liberating others from repressive customs and self-imposed limits. Beauty can be power, and a soul can be its sword, but the key here to remember is that knowledge is power and power is a beautiful thing if used wisely.

CHAPTER 38

Thoughts On Inspiration

"INSPIRE" ALSO MEANS TO BREATHE in. To me, this suggests that enormous amounts of creative and loving force are all around us all of the time. We merely need to recognize this and literally breathe it in to become the best and most compassionate people we can be. Many yogi and meditation practices are based on breathe control. Visualizing, healing, and empowering energy enters the body and mind with each intake of breath, Removing mental debris, negativity, and fear occurs with every exhalation.

If you let it, this world can be a cornucopia of inspiration. Some are inspired by the beauty of nature, of babies and animals and flowers, while others may be inspired by the words and melodies and example of others. I am here, right here and now, because I have been fortunate enough to have the faith, hope, and assistance of loving, caring people in my life. I am inspired by my own rise from the ashes and by the knowledge that my words and my experiences may likewise inspire many others.

Very often, artists and musicians and healers may be at a loss to explain their source of inspiration, but what matters most is that their effectiveness in creating beauty, harmony and health is contagious! I hope my example of rising from abused victim to inspired speaker is contagious too! I sincerely hope that those reading catch the excitement and fervor of self-realization. I want you to know the freedom to grow because a teacher may inspire hope but loving yourself will also help you to grow into your happiest, wisest, and strongest self.

CHAPTER 39

Thoughts On Sex

I ONCE READ THAT ONE should not touch a flower with the intention to pluck it. You should touch the flower intending to nurture it. Sex is soulful. Sex is sacred. Sex is the euphoric coming together of two souls into one. Each partner derives pleasure from the pleasure he or she gives. Sex is a powerful force and should be handled with care. Sigmund Freud described sex as one of the two main drives in human nature. Sex, like all forms of power, can be used for good or bad.

It can be casual, passionate, committed, and even sacred. Ancient wisdom—and practitioners of certain types of yoga—describe the sex force as the kundalini force, which can be dissipated in wasteful and meaningless encounters. Conversely, it can be used to ascend a spiritual pathway toward light, greater wisdom, and deep intimacy with a loving partner. The best sex involves surrender of the ego and the self to an equally trusting partner.

There is sex—and then there is sex. The experience of sexual union with a loved partner is a peak experience, blissful beyond telling. Trust, like love and intimacy, is empowering. If you have ever had the misfortune of being betrayed—and betrayal is the opposite of trust—then you know how affirming and sweet and beautiful loving trust should and can be. Any discussion of sex should involve a discussion of love and relationships as well. It's like putting emotion in motion because for some sex is a beautiful thing if done justly.

CHAPTER 40

Thoughts On Love

WHAT IS LOVE? ALL YOU need is love we kept hearing. Yes, all you need is a little bit of love but do we know how to love? Or at least know the value of love and what it really means? Growing up, I once heard some people say that love is a thing that tickles the heart and upsets the brain. Others say that love is life. We also hear that love is the greatest gift.

Love is not what we say, but how we feel. It is the most powerful force of all, whether we love externally or internally. For me, love is the sweetness of emotions. Internal love results in pleasure. External love is where we say,"She is so sweet" or "He is so sweet." That is external love which then leads to pleasantness, which is joy, and finally, to being adored.

When we love, we open and expand our hearts and spirits to encompass the world and the people around us. When you are in love, whether as a parent, or a partner, or an observer of the wonder and glory of nature, your boundaries expand and you are invulnerable. When the well- being of a loved one means as much or more to you than your own, you have traded the limitations of a single self in a single body for the beauty and ecstatic expression of feeling towards other people. Every time a friend or soldier or parent or partner makes a decision involving some form of self-sacrifice, you see love.

Kindness is also a form of love. It may not cost much or involve great effort to extend a hand or a smile, but in doing so you made the other person's day better and sweeter for it.

As a wise person put it, with every single choice we make, we are either moving toward or away from the goal. Sometimes we must rely on the opinion of others who care about us in recognizing the way we treat people or the way we get treated by other people. We can reinforce love differently. We can first become loved, and then we will recognize the true feelings of what it's like to be loved. Only then can we savor or express love to other people. Just a little appreciation goes a long way. When we value people's feelings and think before we talk, it makes a big difference. Treating someone good is indeed a blessing. My mantra every day is that whatever I do, my work must be praised, and wherever I go, my style is to be admired.

CHAPTER 41

Thoughts On Single Parenting

IN CONTEMPORARY TIMES, BROKEN FAMILIES and divorce have become more the rule rather than the exception. Some children of divorced parents are subjected to tensions and problems that kids in happy homes rarely see. Younger children often misunderstand why mom or dad had to leave, and end up blaming themselves, concluding that they were not lovable enough or did something wrong to cause their parent to leave.

Children of divorce are often subject to "triangulation," a process where one or both parents try to get the child to side with them and to criticize, dislike, and even fear the other parent. Divorced parents are often burdened with guilt, and try to win their child's affection with gifts or by spoiling them. Another common issue is the child's reaction to mom or dad's new friend, who may be a decent and kind person, or a selfish creep jealous of the child's very presence. Help is available in the form of extended families, including close friends, who make it their business to include the child in as many age-appropriate activities as possible, and who act in the way of surrogate parents, such as the kind aunt or uncle.

In situations where the child's well-being is at stake as evidenced by poor school performance, isolation, other unhappy behaviors, counseling can be extremely helpful. There is no reason to expect that a well-loved and appreciated child of divorced parents will not do well in life. All too often, parents who clearly despise each other but stay together for the child's sake harm the child far more than separation and divorce might. Sometimes it is in the child's best interest for warring parents to part.

I grew up separately with my mother, then with my father. When I am with one, I usually miss the other. When living with stepparents, it is easy for a child to say that he is not my father or she is not my mother. However, it doesn't mean all stepparents are evil or harmful. I have a friend whose stepmother treated her with affection and the loving care she never had. I also knew of a stepdad where one could never tell that the kids were not his biological children.

Today, seeing how the world revolves, the good and bad treatment that some children go through is so just or unjust. I got help, and if I can help someone who is going through exactly what I've been through, it is a wonderful thing. Do we ever wonder how hard is it for a single parent? We need to have empathy for someone in that position and be there if they need a shoulder to lean on.

CHAPTER 42

Thoughts On Stress

LIKE IT OR NOT, STRESS is a fact of life. We live in a world of constant change, with people and nations competing with each other for jobs, recognition, and valuable resources. We are bombarded every moment by the television news and reports of war and disaster and crime. Those of us who live in cities must endure a more or less constant soundscape of alarms, sirens, and honking horns.

The workplace is another notorious arena of stress with co-workers competing for promotions, benefits, and recognition. the domestic scene has its own forms of stress, including but not limited to troubled marriages and relationships, school problems, and illness. How do we survive in a world that seems to be accelerating, springing surprises on people, and testing our resiliency with economic, geographic, and political hardship? It's like life has its drastic twist and turns, right?

Coping with stress has become a billion-dollar industry. Bookstores and broadcasts are crammed with experts telling and selling the public on ways to decrease stress in their lives. For me, an important component of reducing stress is knowing yourself.

When you know yourself, you know how to take optimal care of yourself. That means surrounding yourself with positive people, positive energy, and positive pastimes to the fullest extent possible. Knowing yourself also means being aware of the kinds of people and situations that push your buttons. Although rudeness, aggressiveness, competitiveness, and indecency are parts of life, you can always make choices to minimize your exposure to toxic influences.

Set priorities. If you're at your best in peaceful, quiet surroundings, do what you can to position your work and home life to maximize your well-being. Others thrive in a fast-paced, dog-eat-dog environment, and often do well when they can organize their lives and time in such settings.

According to the center for disease control and prevention, everyone—adults, teens, and even children —experiences stress at times. Some stress can be beneficial though. It can help people develop the skills they need to deal with possible threatening situations throughout life. You can put problems into perspective by finding healthy ways to cope. Getting the right care and support can help reduce stressful feelings and symptoms most of the time. Even though some people use different ways when coping with stress, my advice is:

• Take care of yourself first. Eat healthily.
• Exercise regularly.
• Get plenty of sleep.
• Listen to your favorite music.

Most importantly, let your voice be heard and reach out for help, whether it's from a positive friend or pastor or counselor.

CHAPTER 43

Thoughts On Abuse

MY STRUGGLES REQUIRED COURAGE AND determination to survive the cruelty and intolerance of others. Most who go through the vicious cycles of abuse and neglect do not speak out, but I encourage them to do so. Don't hide your stories! Fear breeds more fear; speaking out breeds courage, which leads to strength and more success. My interviews with people have inspired me to speak my story out loud. I now have the courage to push forward. Protecting and saving the vulnerable, the innocent-- children in situations similar to mine--are my source of inspiration. I advocate Zero Tolerance for child abuse or neglect. This message should be publicized and broadcast around the world.

Anything less is neglect or abuse. Abuse is ignored or not reported at least 75% of the time. There are many types of abuse, some worse than others, though all cause serious lasting damage to a life. Abuse can be physical or emotional or both. Eventually, the scars and darkness will show. Children are not the only victims of abuse. Adults and innocent animals suffer unimaginable abuse as well.

Many criminal cases involving abuse go unheard. Many victims continue to suffer as a result. The lasting trauma from abuse has led to many suicides and suicide attempts. No one should have to deal with someone else's rage; no one should have to suffer from its impact.

Abuse in this country is on the rise. Not only here, but worldwide. All people have a right to live free of exploitation and abuse. Everyone in this world is precious, especially you.

My trials have not been easy, but I faced them with strength, courage, and faith. Today, I am an entrepreneur. Guess what? Life, a good life, does not always end with a green card or money or fame. Life is how you make it! For me, life is about one thing: Inner Peace. Only then can one live and lead a sane and productive and creative life. Education is also very important. Education is a major source of inspiration and motivation.

First thing each morning I ask myself, "What kind of day do I wish to have?" Visualize what you want. Growing up with abuse is toxic; hiding pain does nothing but make the scarring worse. If you are a victim of abuse, I urge you to find a way to get your voice heard. That's right; let your voice be heard!

Someone other than you need to know before things get worse. Reaching out sooner rather than later is the key. Abuse is defined as anything that is harmful, injurious or offensive to a person, animal and, for that matter, the environment.

Traumatizing moments will stick like glue. I was subjected to all kinds of abuse only because I loved differently. Don't let fear stop you from speaking out. I encourage you to share what you are facing with someone. Now you know what I had to face. Know that these moments don't last forever. Reach out for help now.

Like the saying goes, "A thousand-mile journey starts with the first step."

All too often, abuse is a problem that only you can solve. Often the only way a victim of abuse can get help is by gathering the courage to speak out and tell someone. It is a well-known fact that millions of people in this country alone are subject to abuse by their parents, their children, their partners, and even by their governments. Anything can and does happen behind closed doors. Child and spouse and elder abuse may go on for years, unrecognized, until a crisis—like a sudden visit to the emergency room— points to a situation of abuse. Abuse can be verbal (insults, put-downs, humiliation, guilt-provoking) or physical, or both. Numerous cases have been documented of women and men reaching out for help, or showing signs of physical abuse, which have either been minimized or totally ignored. In the worst case scenarios, many victims of physical abuse end up crippled or dead. If you or someone you know is a victim of abuse, tell someone! The courage to speak in such a situation can mean the difference between life or death.

CHAPTER 44

Thoughts On Bullying

I WOULD NOT ASK ANYONE to define what bullying is. In fact, bullying is by no means confined to schoolyard mischief. Bullying also occurs in every type of relationship and is carried out by weapons and other methods.

Unhappy partners in discordant power relationships often boss each other around, and have to endure many kinds of strategies—such as unfaithfulness, betrayal, humiliation, tantrums, and physical violence—until one or the other decides to leave, to surrender, or is harmed or killed. Teams, whether athletic or corporate or family, often have a member whose bullying behavior makes life miserable for those around him. We have become more aware in recent years of the catastrophic effect bullying by peers can have on children and adolescents.

Victims of bullies may be too intimidated to tell a parent or teacher about his or her victimhood, and targets of bullies frequently become depressed, isolated, and have even been known in the extreme case to take their lives. According to the American Psychological Association, bullying is a form of aggressive behavior in which someone intentionally and repeatedly causes another person injury or discomfort. One can be bullied in the form of physical contact, words or actions.

The bullied individual typically has trouble defending him or herself and does nothing to cause the bullying. I was once a bullied victim, so I know and feel the pain of someone out there who is being bullied. Today, if someone you know is being bullied, please help them by saying something or helping them find help. Let your voices be heard, make a change, and remember, helping someone today is saving someone's life tomorrow.

CHAPTER 45

Thoughts On Suicide

HAVE YOU EVER THOUGHT OR took the time to appreciate or value the greatest blessing one may have? Life, Life, Life! Suicide is the most extreme form of depression and self- loathing.

If you think about it, suicide is the diametric opposite of self-confidence. Taking your own life is a tragic reaction to stressful life situations because it may seem like there is no way out or no solution to the problem you may be facing. You decided that killing yourself solves everything. A suicidal person has given up on themselves so profoundly that they want to remove themselves from the world.

The wish to not go on living has many causes. Major causes of suicidal thinking and behavior include untreated severe depression, alcohol or drug abuse, sexual orientation disorder, severe and persistent stress. Quite often we may see a handicapped or otherwise challenged person and think, "If I were in that situation, I'd be suicidal too." Wrong! Although loss of a loved one or loss of one's health can be triggers for depression and even suicide, it is vitally important to make a distinction between depression and grieving. With major health issues or the death of a close one, we each go through a period of intense sadness, grief, shock, and even anger. However, normal grief unfolds over time, and the grieving person never loses their interest in life and themselves.

Depression, on the other hand, has a complete loss of interest in the world and in oneself. Sometimes unresolved grief reactions turn into classic depression. Anyone who experiences thoughts of suicide—anyone who would prefer to not go on living— should seek professional help. Friends and relatives of those going through suicidal episodes should take threats of self-harm or cries for help seriously. Hook the suicidal person up with professional help because suicide is treatable. Do you know that suicide can be prevented? I tried suicide twice and often thought about it many times, but getting the help needed is a big plus.

I am here today giving my living testimony that life itself is beautiful and is worthy to be praised. Remember suicidal feelings are temporary. If someone you know is feeling hopeless and doesn't want to live anymore, help them get the treatment that can help them regain their perspective. Life will get better. I urge you always to be supportive to someone for we may not know what that other person is dealing with or what their situation is at hand. We need to respect them whether they are lesbian, gay, bisexual, transgender, or even a confused teenager. It could be someone who is being bullied or suffering from a mental health problem. We have not walked in their shoes, and we should not be quick to judge someone. A little bit of love, caring, and compassion goes a long way.

CHAPTER 46

Thoughts On The Workplace

I GUESS MOST, OR ALL of us has encountered a difficult person we deal with in our workplace. Dealing with jealous co-workers or an unfair supervisor and workplace unpleasantness is a highly personal issue involving a person's core self.

I was persecuted and outcast many times in my workplace. This was based purely on my identity and sexual orientation. People always pass judgment and talk about you. They assume that they know everything about you and want to pass judgment or boss you around or find fault in everything you do. When we encounter these types of negative experiences, I urge you strongly to maintain your focus and stay in the moment of remembering that your voice can be heard and there is justice out there. No one should be subjected to any type of abuse or workplace hate. On the other hand, it is said that we spend most of our time at our job, and we should treat the people in the workplace as family.

There are always some colleagues you trust; someone to turn to for advice or opinions. In my experience, I always turn to the ones that are very enthusiastic, positive, and loyal. I always turn to people that I gained knowledge from instead of gossiping with. Sticking with positive people brings positive feedback, and positive feedback leads to success which leads to prosperity. Trusting someone, and to be trusted, is always greater than being loved. Choose who you trust and make wise decisions.

CHAPTER 47

Thoughts On Determination

DETERMINATION IS ANOTHER KEY TO achieving your goal. The steely determination to succeed is the cousin of persistence. Don't let disappointments get in your way. Take the long view that a bad day is not an occasion for despair, but a mere blip on the radar screen of your life and your long term goals. Sometimes you will lose a battle, but with determination, persistence, and the help of good people, you will win the war. Wear yourself and your individuality with pride. Instead of trying to fit in, distinguish yourself and enhance your dignity by standing out. Your choices, your decisions, and your goals are worthy of respect from you and from others.

Likewise, recognize when the actions and accomplishment of others excel and deserve your respect. They say the pen is mightier than the sword; I say words are equally potent, for good or ill. Many people will tell you about something a respected teacher, adult, or other authority figure once said that changed the course of their life. If it wasn't for the compassion and generosity of the elderly black woman who approached me as I sat there sobbing on a park bench and suggested that I seek political asylum in the United States, I might still be a slave to the primitive ways of my native land.

Take risks. Remember: nothing ventured, nothing gained. Once you've thought it through, take calculated risks at work, in relationships, and in life. Either you will succeed, or you will have the gratification of knowing that you did what you could to make things better.

CHAPTER 48

Thoughts On Success

WHAT IS SUCCESS? ASK ONE hundred people, and you're likely to get one hundred different answers. To me, the most successful people are those who know what they really and truly want, who know who they are, and who have been fortunate enough to enjoy the process of getting there.

I personally don't measure success by the size of a bank account or an expensive car. Success to me is getting up after a fall, the motivation to achieve a goal, or to fight and finally have a desire fulfilled. Success can be defined in many different ways such as waking up every day and being grateful for life itself. Having good health is success because, with great health, we can achieve everything as we journey in this life.

The pathway to success begins with what makes you happy and going after that journey, fight hard and push toward that goal, and winning it with great achievement. Someone living in poverty can be very successful when he or she finds contentment. So, we should never measure success based on wealth or fortune or fame. When aiming for success, we should first ask ourselves, does this truly matter to me? What do I want to achieve? What are your weakness and your strength and, most importantly, is this the right path for you? Remember knowing who you are and wanting what you want while working for it with great determination will bring you success.

CHAPTER 49

Getting Better All The Time

I WANT TO FINISH UP with my story with a referral from my attorney, I reached out and began to piece the puzzles of my inner self together with psychological help. I wanted to face my fears and mend all of me and become one whole person, one whole self.

There is danger in living without facing our demons. Knowing this helped me tremendously as I went from doctor to doctor for help. I received much love and felt grateful every step of the way.

I felt a little stronger each day. I didn't need to be institutionalized in a psychiatric ward. I was strong enough to face the many challenges that I had and honest enough to reach out for the help that I needed.

Although I had much pain, I chose to pick myself up and not allow the weight of the world to drag me down. Being an inspiration to others is one of my main motivations now. Giving advice and suggestions to clients in the salon only drew people closer to me. Everyone has a story to tell, just like the scars on my body. More and more people looked up to me for support and guidance.

Receiving my degree as a surgical technologist was the icing on the cake. As a surgical technologist you assist with the surgeries in the operating room. Maintaining sterility and anticipating a surgeon's needs in the operating room is essential. Being human by remaining in the moment and maintaining focus is very rewarding as well.

From the beginning, I knew that I wanted to to do something more than run a beauty salon. Doing my research online, I ran across the words *lab technician*.

So many conflicting thoughts ran through my mind. I asked myself, *"At this age, could I honestly fulfill the qualifications and concentrate on my studies, especially science?"*

I also came across the words, *surgical technologist*. Right away I knew this was it: this would be the place for me. I was highly fascinated by every aspect of the operating room after undergoing surgery myself. My dream was to assist a surgeon and assist in the life-and-death world of the operating room.

I got my degree and began to work in the field, a very happy employee. It felt good knowing I had graduated with a college degree, motivating me even further to expand my education in the future.

Like most girls, I would like to get married and have lots of children one day. I hope to give my kids the love that I never had.

My life in Richmond Hill in Queens, NY, is not bad at all. Like anywhere, it has its problems too. This place makes me think of home, of how provincial it was. I have received much respect and admiration. Of course, I still have moments of discrimination from narrow-minded people who notice the transition.

Such moments no longer bother me, but the thought of what others may go through does. Many people need education, need to have their awareness level raised regarding abuse of all kinds. This society can no longer afford ignorance and intolerance. It is sinful and dead wrong to bash and abuse those who are perceived as different.

I know of the murder of many men, women, and children. I want this put to a stop. Regardless of what others may think, I consider myself a woman of dignity who is worthy of respect and praise.

My studies are a work in progress. I still hope to pursue other surgical areas.

"There is nothing like a mother's love," is the bottom line for me. The statement is true and real and always holds its weight. My mother migrated to the United States six years ago. She has been one of my major support systems along this journey of transition. I love and honor my mother, just as any newborn would.

Not only do I have her support, but I now have the support of my grandparents and the rest of my family every step of the way. It amazes me how the relationships with my family have grown, how good it feels to have them by my side. My family now spends a lot of time with me. My cousins show me great respect and, in fact, look up to me an elder.

I give thanks to those friends that I gained and those who have given me loyalty and trust along the way. I did not depend on them as much as they would have allowed, but I am deeply thankful for their presence, which helped me overcome the obstacles in my way.

I started to expand my life and had the privilege of meeting other artists and actors in the community. Organizations did open my mind to more possibilities and had my story featured in a play, *Tara's Crossing*.

The play was well received in schools. It highlights the immigration and detention situations around the U.S. *Tara's Crossing* has played in many colleges across the country to illustrate struggles like mine.

It was an inspiration to me and was produced to give inspiration to others, especially when I was present and offered advocacy and support in the after-show talks that followed each performance.

I decided to share my life story with The Caribbean Equality Project. The Caribbean Equality Project focuses on advancing social change in everyday life, on making people more aware, and on inspiring the community. This too has proven to be a good platform for advocating change.

I was also interviewed in one of the installments of the "Self-Made Successful Women." I got to answer questions about myself and my somewhat unique story. I got to describe how I had bettered my life.

The first question directed at me was, "What is your definition of success?"

I replied, "My definition of success is about getting back on your feet after failure or getting up after a fall. As a survivor of torture, keeping a desire reach a goal is indeed a kind of success to me. My daily routine is always prayers. Being spiritual helped me a lot, especially with finding out more about who I am and what I was going through. I have been on a vegan diet for 14 years. My biggest challenge was being born different, and I wanted to heal myself because my body said one thing while my mind said another. My advice to younger people who are going through what I went through is you are not alone, and *I know your pain*. I may not have experienced the same torture as you but believe me, I've been there. Nothing is permanent, not even pain. It can just be temporary, especially in today's fast-moving world. Your voice can be heard so let your voice be heard. Please let your voice be heard because only you have that power to make a change and make a difference."

This quote is the mantra I live by. Wherever I go and whatever I do, I always try to give it my best, so that my work will be praised and my style admired. I want to show that if one believes and has the hope of faith, people can make it through whatever they may be facing on their journey.

Keep fighting with determination in your heart and accept who you are. At the end of the day, I believe we all have a strong desire for inner peace and should give ourselves such peace every day!

The life I live now? I spend it watching *Lifetime* stories that influence my daily deeds. These shows inspire me to push ahead in my faith and everyday living.

Lifetime has its commercial side, but my focus is on the good that they do with their daily broadcasts. My story is a prime example of there being a light at the end of the tunnel.

You cannot give up; you must remain strong-willed to make it out of your situation. You must love yourself first, then anything is possible.

Anything is possible.

Things in my life have gotten better and better. I have been approached and asked out on dates by men in high society, including doctors, lawyers, and even police officers.

This next story is about one of my dates and the closest that came towards becoming another actual relationship.

I decided to go on a date with Doctor Lee.

Coming close to love was a beautiful thing for me. The doctor had another friend, Dr. Schwartz, who was a co-worker. Both are oral maxillofacial surgeons, and I ended up going on three dates with Dr. Schwartz as well.

It might sound bad, or self-indulgent, but my dating life was quite wild. I admit it. I enjoyed the wining and the dining at almost every expensive restaurant in New York City.

This was very exciting for me, navigating through life's sometimes funny, sometimes tangled situations. As it turned out, Doctor Schwartz was married, though. I certainly could not blame myself for that. As they say, "If you knew better, you would do better."

These episodes were transient, ephemeral. Lee was the guy that I had developed feelings for before all this occurred, and my longing for him escalated quickly. He was one of those surgeons who got what he wanted, when he wanted it, and with whomever he wanted it with.

I was deeply attracted to him. He caught my eye before the friend ever did. Call me crazy, but I was still dating Dr. Schwartz, his friend. On a day to day basis, Lee and I would work beside each other, mostly during surgeries. Through this, we grew closer and more attached to one another.

We made eye contact at every opportunity, luring one another in deeper and deeper. Feeling his gloves against mine as we worked surgical cases only upped the ante.

A connection was undoubtedly there. Sooner or later this would lead to something. Hopefully, some kind of commitment, at least as far I was concerned. All this eye contact, the inadvertent touch of hands - these kind of events usually lead to a date. The question was, did he know?

Did he know about me and my change? What if he found out?

I had hidden it for all this time, and this might cause him to turn on me and put a halt to what was happening between us.

I could not take more disappointment, could not endure another heartbreak. Still, I took the chance, and I will tell the next man I fall in love with about my true self.

First, though, I have to make sure he is someone who deserves my love and trust.

After many begging pleading phone calls from Dr. Lee, I agreed to go on some casual dates with him. He was not all that appealing.

His breath smelled bad, he was possessive, and he wanted to control me. He had psoriasis, which he did not take care of. He worked out a lot, but that didn't validate his need to feel that he was is in charge of everyone and everything all the time.

His friend Dr. Schwartz tried to warn me about his controlling behavior, but I guess I had to experience it for myself. I should not be fearing Lee's power over me just because of his elevated status in society. People in power - authority figures like a police officer, a doctor, even the president - should practice extra empathy and kindness, not provoke fear.

In fact, I greatly respect them, but what matters at the end of the day is being a human who serves humanity. Only then can one know inner peace and gain the respect of others.

I was still rejoicing at my change in fortune by going on dates with Dr. Schwartz or occasionally going locally with friends for happy hour or dinner while exploring NYC.

That is when Dr. Patel, an anesthesiologist at the same hospital, saw me and said that he was crazy about me. He wanted to take me out. He very much wanted to take me out. We exchanged phone numbers, and he kept on asking me out. I asked him for some time to think about it. He claimed that he had eyes for me for months and was attracted to me but had been too shy to approach me about his situation. He was considerably younger than me. He was hot. He was tall, dark and good-looking, an Indian hunk of a doctor.

After a day or two, he started contacting me again, but I wanted to keep it casual. My anxiety about disclosing my change still had the upper hand. Speaking of the name Patel, I have to go to the mall because I need powder and mascara for my date at the the movies tonight with another Dr. Patel. Yes, a second Dr. Patel who like Patel #1 was also an anesthesiologist.

It looks like I may end up with one Dr. Patel or another, but hey, you never know what life holds in store. We met during happy hour at a bar where he introduced himself to me. Walked right up to ask if I was a model because I looked and walked like one. He was mesmerized by my look and by my 5-inch heels.

I asked him if he had modeling connections, and we became very close friends over time. He was not the first man who proposed modeling.

This doctor (Patel #2) and I became good friends. Very good friends. He was older and hoped for something intimate in the future, but I kept it as just friends. He was going through a divorce and claimed that his wife cheated on him repeatedly. I was always there for him.

I am glad he trusts me as a friend, glad that he had someone – me - to lean on. I gave him advice and tried to make him feel positive about his future. He listened carefully to all my criticisms and suggestions. He had court the following day for the final decision on custody of his three children.

He was a doctor and a professional, yet he was scared, never having faced a judge before. My thoughts returned to December 1, 2003, when I appeared in immigration court for my final decision.

The judge was very tough, being an immigrant herself. I was especially scared because she was said to deport and deny peoples' applications to stay in the U.S. Maybe the rumor was wrong. Maybe she hated having to deport immigrants.

That morning, as I arrived at the courthouse with my attorney and my grandmother at my side, the judge started hearing cases. Soon enough, it was my turn. I entered alone with my lawyer. As my lawyer submitted the supporting documents, the judge called me up to the witness stand.

The judge was about 5 feet, 7 inches tall. I turned to face the clock. My heart raced, considerably faster than the ticking of the clock. My fate was in the hands of this grey-haired, brown-skinned judge.

She leafed through the papers while thinking about her decision. I grew numb watching this judge quietly weigh my future.

Oh, my God! What if she denied my application for political asylum? My heart beat harder and harder.

After looking through all the papers, the judge asked me two questions. I felt like the dark brown walls of the courtroom would come crashing down on top of me. I started to shiver and perspire heavily, all at the same time.

"Defendant! Tell me, what did you think the reason was that you were persecuted and attacked in your home country? And how would you feel and what would you do if you are granted asylum, knowing that you will not be able to travel back to Guyana if something should happen to your mother or brothers?" she bellowed.

"Your Honor," I began, "my mother would be very happy to know that I am safe and that's very important to her. I was subjected to abuse, to rape, and I was beaten, stabbed, burnt, and even stoned just because of who I am. You see, since I was five years old, I have always felt like a girl even though I wasn't born as one. These feelings became stronger as I grew up even though I visited many doctors over the years. I went to Dr. Delamita and Dr. Sheere, who are both endocrinologists specializing in hormonal therapies. The doctors kept saying that I was born with more female hormones than male hormones and strongly recommended sexual reassignment surgery, a sex change."

Her fixed, stern glare offered little comfort, but I did not despair. I couldn't read her thoughts. Her countenance betrayed little of what she was thinking or how she would rule.

"Being born in a third world country filled with ignorance and bigotry, it was hard and painful for me, and it invited persecution and torture upon my life," I continued. "So today, as a transgendered woman, I am seeking political asylum based on my gender identity and imputed sexual orientation."

After hearing this, the judge made her final decision.

"In the matter of Veemala Persaud, a male who strongly looks like a girl and identifies as one. This application for asylum is..."

CHAPTER 50

Life Goes On

TODAY, I AM IN A safer place. My life has been a roller coaster ride with its ups and downs and twists and turns. I survived terrible ordeals and a state of constant fear yet I was eventually able to spring back and enjoy things and to get on with my life.

The prisons of the past – my father's house, my aunt and uncle's domination, the men of my country – are behind me now and can no longer do me harm.

I am free. One taste of freedom and there was no going back. Some still try to denounce me, even now. They show up when I do motivational speeches or after I am on a video speaking out against abuse.

They verbally assault me, trying to put me back in that prison, but there is no going back. Many people condemn me by quoting the Holy Bible. The Holy Bible also mentions that if a man or a woman conceive out of wedlock they should be stoned to death. Jesus also said that whoever is born without sin should cast the first stone at a sinner. So what makes me an abomination before the Lord?

The learning experiences have made me tough - Army strong. Who was it who once said, "Whatever doesn't kill me outright makes me stronger?"I have fought a fight that many did not survive, but my survival and my story are gifts given to me to share with you.

I am still growing each day, trying to be the best person I can. I hope that reading this will help you because this is truly why we are here - to help each other, to unite.

My accomplishments reveal what is reachable to you. Never put a limit on what you can do. Simply show how much you can achieve, and then some! Far too often we let our external environment or ourselves put a limit to what we can do. We are always capable of more! I am a living witness to that. Endurance, patience, and faith make almost anything possible.

My family life has improved considerably. I now have much closer relationships with my aunts who live in America. My mother continues to be my source of inspiration. My little brother will soon be a graduate from college.

The family members who are close to me now accept me, and I welcome their love. It is the love I searched for as a child and have now found as an adult. My mother, who I remember looking so small at the hands of my father's abuse, proved to me what *real* strength was. She lived through so much abuse, sickness, and poverty. Yet, she persevered through it all. Because of that strength, she was able to come to America and see me graduate from school. Strength comes in all shapes and sizes.

There are many lessons I cannot put on the blackboard of those going through trials similar to mine. I have reached out to many lives and hope for more opportunities to speak and inspire and motivate others.

Most who go through the vicious cycles of abuse and neglect do not speak out, but I encourage them to speak out. Don't hide your stories! Fear breeds more fear; speaking out breeds courage, which leads to strength and more success.

My interviews with people throughout the city have further inspired me to speak my story out loud. I now have the courage to push forward. Protecting and saving the vulnerable, the innocent children in situations similar to mine are my source of inspiration. I advocate ZERO TOLERANCE for child abuse or neglect.

This message should be publicized; should be broadcast around the world.

Anything less is neglect or abuse.

Abuse is ignored or not reported at least 75% of the time. There are many types of abuse, some worse than others, though all cause serious lasting damage to a life.

Abuse can be physical or emotional or both. Eventually, the scars and darkness will show children are not the only victims of abuse. Adults and innocent animals suffer unimaginable abuse as well.

Criminal cases involving abuse go unheard. Many continue to suffer as a result. The lasting trauma from abuse has led to many suicides and suicide attempts.

No one should have to deal with someone else's rage; no one should have to suffer from its impact.

Abuse in this country is on the rise. Not just in America but worldwide. All people have a right to live free of exploitation and abuse.

Everyone in this world is precious. I learned that during my journey to the United States. My trials have not been easy, but I faced them with strength and courage and even faith.

Any women, man, or child could have face what I did as my dad was alcoholic and my mother was abused. I was subjected to child labor and child abuse and above all, fighting with my desired feelings and dealing with LGBT issues.

Today, I am an entrepreneur. And guess what? Life, a good life, does not always end with a green card or money or fame.

Life is how you make it! Life is about one thing: INNER PEACE. Only then can one live and lead a sane and productive and creative life.

Education is also very important. Education is a major source of inspiration and motivation.

First thing each morning I ask myself, what kind of day do I wish to have? Visualize what you really want.

Growing up with abuse is toxic. Hiding pain does nothing but makes the scarring worse.

If you are a victim of abuse, find a way to get your voice heard. Someone other than you need to know before things get worse.

Reaching out sooner rather than later is the key. *Abuse* is defined as anything that is harmful, injurious, or offensive to a person, animal and, for that matter, the environment.

You may be a victim of physical abuse or mental abuse. Or both. Traumatizing moments will stick like glue. I was subjected to all kinds of abuse because I loved differently.

Don't let **fear** stop you from speaking out.

I encourage you to share what you are facing with someone you trust.

Now you know what I had to face. Know that these moments don't last forever. Reach out for help now.

RESOURCES

Child Abuse

CHILDREN'S BUREAU

Administration for Children and Families
U.S. Department of Health & Human Services
330 C Street, S.W.
Washington, D.C. 20201

The Children's Bureau (CB) partners with federal, state, tribal and local agencies to improve the overall health and well-being of our nation's children and families and offers the following programs:

- **Promoting Safe and Stable Families**
- **The Court Improvement program**
- **Child Abuse Prevention and Treatment Act (CAPTA)**
- **CAPTA discretionary fund**
- **CAPTA state grants**
- **Community-Based Child Abuse Prevention (CBCAP) Grants**
- **The Children's Justice Act (CJA)**

- **National Conferences on Child Abuse & Neglect**

CHILD WELFARE INFORMATION GATEWAY

1-800=394-3366
info@childwelfare.gov
Providing the following list of resources:

ARCH National Respite Network and Resource Center

4016 Oxford Street
Annandale, Virginia 22003
Phone: (703) 256-9578

The mission of the ARCH National Respite Network and Resource Center is to assist and promote the development of quality respite and crisis care programs; to help families locate respite and crisis care services in their communities; and to serve as a strong voice for respite in all forums.

Resources: Child Abuse (continued)
American Academy of Pediatrics

345 Park Boulevard
National Headquarters
Itasca, Illinois 60143
Phone: (202) 247-8600
Phone: (800) 433-9016
Fax: (202) 393-6137, (847) 434-8000
Email: kidsdocs@aap.org

The **Healthy Children** website offers tips and training for parents on a variety of issues such as safety and injury prevention, mental health, and child development. For more information, see http://www.healthychildren.org/.

American Professional Society on the Abuse of Children

1706 E. Broad Street
Columbus, Ohio 43203
Phone: (614) 827-1321
Toll-Free: (877) 402-7722
Fax: (614) 251-6005
Email: apsac@apsac.org
http://www.apsac.org

General Scope: The American Professional Society on the Abuse of Children (APSAC) addresses all facets of the professional response to child maltreatment: prevention, assessment, intervention, and treatment.

American Psychological Association

750 First Street, NE
Washington, District of Columbia 20002
Phone: (202) 336-5500
Toll-Free: (800) 374-2721
https://www.apa.org

The APA Violence Prevention Office (VPO) coordinates APA's activities related to violence and injury prevention, and treatment on topics associated with child maltreatment, trauma, media violence, and youth violence. VPO major functions are: (a) Coordination of the development, implementation, and

Resources: Child Abuse (continued)

evaluation of two major programs: the ACT/Raising Safe Kids Program (parenting skills training and child maltreatment prevention program) and The Effective Providers for Child Victims of Violence Program (training for mental health and other professionals on trauma, assessment tools and treatment models for children victimized by violence); (b) Development of training and educational materials, technical assistance and training to professionals and organizations participating in both programs; (c) Dissemination of research-based knowledge, information, and materials to professionals and the general public on violence, prevention and related topics through Web (www.actagainstviolence.apa.org), Facebook page www.Facebook.com/ACTRaisingSafeKids and other social media outlets; (d) Collaboration with other national associations, national collaboratives, and federal agencies to promote the contributions of psychology and psychologists to the understanding and prevention of violence.

Annie E. Casey Foundation

701 St. Paul Street
Baltimore, Maryland 21202
Phone: (410) 547-6600
Fax: (410) 547-6624
https://www.facebook.com/AnnieECaseyFndn?ref=ts
https://twitter.com/aecfnews
http://www.youtube.com/user/AnnieECaseyFound

The Annie E. Casey Foundation works to build better futures for disadvantaged children and their families. The primary mission of the Foundation is to foster public policies, human service reforms, and community supports that meet the needs of today's vulnerable children and families.

Center for the Study of Social Policy

1575 Eye Street NW
Suite 500
Washington, District of Columbia 20005
Phone: (202) 371-1565
Fax: (202) 371-1472
http://www.cssp.org/
https://www.facebook.com/pages/Center-for-the-Study-of-Social-Policy/119688008090715

https://twitter.com/CtrSocialPolicy

The mission of the Center for the Study of Social Policy (CSSP) is to develop and promote public policies and practices that support and strengthen families and help communities produce equal opportunities and better futures for children.

The Center coordinates the national Strengthening Families initiative which is being implemented in over half of all States. Strengthening Families engages early childhood programs and other unusual partners

Resources: Child Abuse (continued)

in preventing child abuse and neglect by building five, research-based, Protective Factors that are shown to be correlated with reduced incidence of child abuse and neglect. The Strengthening Families National Network provides tools, peer support, technical assistance, and other resources for States implementing Strengthening Families. For more information about this initiative, please see http://www. strengtheningfamilies.net

Chapin Hall Center for Children

1313 East 60th Street
Chicago, Illinois 60637
Phone: (773) 256-5100
Fax: (773) 753-5940
http://www.chapinhall.org/

Chapin Hall is a research and development center focusing on policies, practices, and programs affecting children and the families and communities in which they live. The Center devotes special attention to children facing significant problems such as abuse or neglect, poverty, and mental or physical illnesses, and to the service systems designed to address these problems.

Child Welfare Information Gateway

Children's Bureau/ACYF
330 C Street, S.W
Washington, District of Columbia 20201
Toll-Free: (800) 394-3366
Email: info@childwelfare.gov
http://www.childwelfare.gov
https://www.facebook.com/childwelfare

Child Welfare Information Gateway connects professionals and the general public to information and resources targeted to the safety, permanency, and well-being of children and families.

A service of the Children's Bureau, Administration for Children and Families, U.S. Department of Health and Human Services, Child Welfare Information Gateway provides access to programs, research, laws and policies, training resources, statistics, and much more.

Child Welfare League of America

Headquarters
727 15th St. NW
12th Floor

Resources: Child Abuse (continued)

Washington, District of Columbia 20005
Phone: (202) 688-4200
Fax: (202) 833-1689
Email: cwla@cwla.org
http://www.cwla.org/
https://www.facebook.com/CWLAUpdates

The Child Welfare League of America (CWLA) is the oldest national organization serving vulnerable children, youth, and their families. CWLA provides training, consultation, and technical assistance to child welfare professionals and agencies while also educating the public on emerging issues that affect abused, neglected, and at-risk children. Through its publications, conferences, and teleconferences, CWLA shares information on emerging trends, specific topics in child welfare practice (family foster care, kinship care, adoption, positive youth development), and Federal and State policies.

Childhelp®

4350 E. Camelback Rd.
Bldg F250
Phoenix, Arizona 85018

Phone: (480) 922-8212
Toll-Free: (800) 4AC-HILD
TDD: (800) 2AC-HILD
Fax: (480) 922-7061
http://www.childhelp.org/
https://www.facebook.com/childhelp
https://twitter.com/Childhelp
http://www.youtube.com/childhelponline

Childhelp® is dedicated to helping victims of child abuse and neglect. Childhelp's approach focuses on prevention, intervention and treatment. The Childhelp National Child Abuse Hotline, 1-800-4-A-CHILD®, operates 24 hours a day, seven days a week, and receives calls from throughout the United States, Canada, the U.S. Virgin Islands, Puerto Rico and Guam. Childhelp's programs and services also include residential treatment services; children's advocacy centers; therapeutic foster care; group homes; child abuse prevention, education and training; and the National Day of Hope®, part of National Child Abuse Prevention Month every April.

Resources: Child Abuse (continued)
Circle of Parents

P.O. Box 17982
Richmond, Virginia 23226
Phone: (540) 847-8483
Phone: (804) 308-0841
Email: Circleofparentsac@gmail.com
http://www.circleofparents.org

The mission of the Circle of Parents is to prevent child abuse and neglect and to strengthen families through friendly, supportive, mutual self-help parent support groups and children's programs.

Currently the Circle of Parents national network represents a partnership of parent leaders and 26 statewide organizations in 25 States and Puerto Rico. The organization was formed after a successful collaborative project of Prevent Child Abuse America and the National Family Support Roundtable, which was made possible by the Children's Bureau, Administration on Children, Youth and Families, U.S. Department of Health and Human Services.

The Circle of Parents website provides links to information about the program model, its state network member organizations, training and technical assistance to its membership, parenting resources, and more.

Darkness to Light

7 Radcliffe Street
Suite 200
Charleston, South Carolina 29403
Phone: (843) 965-5444
Toll-Free: (866) FOR-LIGH T8663675444
Fax: (843) 965-5449
http://www.darkness2light.org/
https://www.facebook.com/DarknessToLight
https://twitter.com/darkness2light

Darkness to Light is a primary prevention program whose mission is to engage adults in the prevention of child sexual abuse; to reduce the incidence of child sexual abuse nationally through education and public awareness aimed at adults; and to provide adults with information to recognize and react responsibly to child sexual abuse.

Resources: Child Abuse (continued)

Doris Duke Charitable Foundation

650 Fifth Avenue, 19th Floor
New York, New York 10019
Phone: (212) 974-7000
Fax: (212) 974-7590

The mission of the Doris Duke Charitable Foundation's Child Abuse Prevention Program is to protect children from abuse and neglect in order to promote their healthy development.

The program awards grants to organizations to improve parent-child interactions and to increase parents' access to information and services that help prevent child maltreatment before it occurs.

FRIENDS National Center for Community-Based Child Abuse Prevention (CBCAP)

800 Eastowne Drive
Suite 105
Chapel Hill, North Carolina 27514
Phone: (919) 493-1584
http://friendsnrc.org/

FRIENDS National Center for Community-Based Child Abuse Prevention (CBCAP) is a program authorized by Title II of the Child Abuse Prevention and Treatment Act that provides Federal funds to a lead agency in each State designated by the Governor to provide leadership for and support to child abuse prevention programs and activities in the State. FRIENDS assists CBCAP State Lead Agencies meet the requirements of their funding through the development of written resources and the provision of training and technical assistance.

Gundersen National Child Protection Training Center

175 West Mark Street
Maxwell Hall, 2nd Floor
Winona, Minnesota 55987
Phone: (614) 834-7946
http://www.gundersenhealth.org/ncptc

The Gundersen National Child Protection Training Center (NCPTC) works to end child abuse, neglect and other forms of child maltreatment in three generations through education, training, awareness, prevention, advocacy and the pursuit of justice. The Center promotes reformation of current training practices by providing an educational curriculum to current and future front-line child protection professionals around the nation so that they will be prepared to recognize and report the abuse of a child. NCPTC also focuses on prevention, advocacy, and education through the Jacob Wetterling

Resources: Child Abuse (continued)

Resource Center, the Center for Effective Discipline, and the National Association to Prevent the Sexual Abuse of Children. test

National Alliance of Children's Trust and Prevention Funds

5712 30th Avenue NE
Seattle, Washington 98105
Phone: (206) 526-1221
Fax: (206) 526-0220
Email: info@ctfalliance.org

The National Alliance of Children's Trust and Prevention Funds (ACT) initiates and engages in national efforts that assist state Children's Trust and Prevention Funds in strengthening families to prevent child abuse and neglect. This includes promoting and supporting a system of services, laws, practices, and attitudes that supports families by enabling them to provide their children with a safe, healthy, and nurturing childhood.

National Association for the Education of Young Children

1509 16th Street NW
Washington, District of Columbia 20036
Phone: (202) 232-8777
Toll-Free: (800) 424-2460
Fax: (202) 328-1846
Email: naeyc@naeyc.org
http://www.naeyc.org/
https://www.facebook.com/NAEYC
https://twitter.com/naeyc

The National Association for the Education of Young Children (NAEYC) is the leading membership association for those working with and on behalf of children from birth through age 8.

NAEYC convenes thought leaders, teachers and other practitioners, researchers, and other stakeholders and sets standards of excellence for programs and teachers in early childhood education. NAEYC members include teachers, paraeducators, center directors, trainers, college educators, families of young children, and the public at large. Membership is open to all individuals who share a desire to serve and act on behalf of the needs and rights of all young children.

Resources: Child Abuse (continued)
National Center for Children in Poverty

215 West 125th Street 3rd Floor
154 Haven Avenue
New York, New York 10027
Phone: (646) 284-9600
Fax: (646) 284-9623
http://www.nccp.org/

The National Center for Children in Poverty (NCCP) is a public policy center dedicated to promoting the economic security, health, and well-being of America's low income families and children. Using research to inform policy and practice, NCCP seeks to advance family-oriented solutions and the strategic use of public resources at the State and national levels to ensure positive outcomes for the next generation.

National Center on Shaken Baby Syndrome

1433 North Highway 1075 West
Suite 110
Farmington, Utah 84025
Phone: (801) 447-9360
Fax: (801) 447-9364
Email: mail@dontshake.org
http://www.dontshake.org/

General Scope: The National Center on Shaken Baby Syndrome (NCSBS) offers information on shaken baby syndrome, shaken baby syndrome prevention programs, and training for professionals and parents nationwide.

National Child Abuse & Neglect Technical Assistance and Strategic Dissemination Center (CANTASD) @Impaq International

4350 East West Highway
Suite 1100
Bethesda, Maryland 20814
Phone: 240-744-7071
Email: hello@cantasd.org
http://www.cantasd.org/index.html

The National Child Abuse and Neglect Technical Assistance and Strategic Dissemination Center (CANTASD) is a service of the Children's Bureau, Office on Child Abuse & Neglect. Its focus is the "front

Resources: Child Abuse (continued)

end" of the child welfare system, creating resources and supporting peer learning activities—including the National Conferences on Child Abuse & Neglect—for those engaged in primary and secondary prevention, child protective services and investigation, and multidisciplinary and interagency collaborations to promote the safety and well-being of children, youth, and families.

National Children's Alliance

516 C Street, NE
Washington, District of Columbia 20002
Phone: (202) 548-0090
Toll-Free: (800)239-9950
Fax: (202) 548-0099
http://www.nationalchildrensalliance.org/

https://www.facebook.com/NationalChildrensAlliance

General Scope: The National Children's Alliance is a nonprofit membership organization that provides training, technical assistance, and networking opportunities to communities seeking to plan, establish, and improve Children's Advocacy Centers. These Centers further the goal of serving abused children through a comprehensive approach to services for victims and their families.

National Court Appointed Special Advocate Association

100 West Harrison Street
North Tower, Suite 500
Seattle, Washington 98119
Phone: (206) 774-7250
Toll-Free: (800) 628-3233
http://www.CASAforChildren.org
https://www.facebook.com/CASAforChildren
https://twitter.com/NationalCASA
http://www.youtube.com/casaforchildren

Court Appointed Special Advocates (CASA) for Children is a network of 933 community-based programs that recruit, train and support citizen-volunteers to advocate for the best interests of abused and neglected children in courtrooms and communities. Volunteer advocates—empowered directly by the courts—offer judges the critical information they need to ensure that each child's rights and needs are being attended to while in foster care.

Resources: Child Abuse (continued)
National Fatherhood Initiative

12410 Milestone Center Drive
Suite 600
Germantown, Maryland 20874
Phone: (301) 948-0599
Fax: (301) 948-6776
https://twitter.com/thefatherfactor

The National Fatherhood Initiative works to improve the well-being of children by increasing the proportion of children growing up with involved, responsible, and committed fathers.

National Indian Child Welfare Association

5100 SW Macadam Avenue
Suite 300
Portland, Oregon 97239
Phone: (503) 222-4044
Email: info@nicwa.org
http://www.nicwa.org

https://www.facebook.com/NativeChildren?v=feed& story_fbid=111114601179

https://twitter.com/NativeChildren

The National Indian Child Welfare Association (NICWA) functions as the only Native American organization focused specifically on issues of child abuse and neglect and tribal capacity to prevent and respond effectively to these problems. NICWAprovide workshops and training programs, using culturally appropriate NICWA developed resources, including training materials, curricula, and books. NICWA also offers technical assistance and training on child care, family preservation, and substance abuse.

National Network of Family Support and Strengthening Networks

95 Washburn Street
San Francisco, California 94103
Phone: (415) 730-5310
Email: info@nationalfamilysupportnetwork.org
https://nationalfamilysupportnetwork.org/

Founded in 2011, the National Network of Family Support & Strengthening Networks (NNFSSN) is a membership-based organization comprised of statewide networks that focus on strengthening and

Resources: Child Abuse (continued)

supporting families. Each of these networks consists of two or more Family Resource Centers or Family Strengthening organizations. The mission of the NNFSSN is to connect statewide networks across the United States to promote quality practice, peer learning, mutual support, and effective policies and systems that support positive outcomes for children, families, and communities.

National Resource Center for Healthy Marriage and Families

9300 Lee Highway
Fairfax, Virginia 22031

Toll-Free: 1-866-916-4672
Email: info@HealthyMarriageandFamilies.org

The National Resource Center for Healthy Marriage
and Families promotes the value of healthy marriage and
relationship education (MRE) skills and encourages their
integration into safety-net service systems as a holistic
approach to strengthening families.

Nurse-Family Partnership

1900 Grant Street
Suite 400
Denver, Colorado 80203
Phone: (303) 327-4240
Toll-Free: (866) 864-5226
Fax: (303) 327-4260
Email: info@nursefamilypartnership.org
http://www.nursefamilypartnership.org/

The Nurse-Family Partnership represents an approach to
the long-established service strategy of the home visiting
model that improves the health and social functioning of low
income, first-time mothers, their babies, and families.

Parents Anonymous® Inc.

675 West Foothill Boulevard
Suite 220
Claremont, California 91711-3475
Phone: (909) 621-6184
Fax: (909) 625-6304
Email: Parentsanonymous@parentsanonymous.org
http://www.parentsanonymous.org

Resources: Child Abuse (continued)

https://www.facebook.com/NationalParentHelpline
https://twitter.com/parenthelpline
http://www.youtube.com/parenthelpline

Parents Anonymous® Inc. is a family strengthening organization dedicated to the prevention of child abuse and neglect. Parents Anonymous® Inc. operates numerous programs and initiatives, including an international **Network** of accredited organizations that implement Parents Anonymous® groups and complementary children and youth programs based on a mutual support-shared leadership® model. In addition, Parents Anonymous ® provides many services, including specialized trainings, customized technical assistance, public awareness and outreach strategies, and evaluation services to States, counties, and community-based organizations on a wide range of topics related to children and families.

Prevent Child Abuse America

228 S. Wabash
10th Floor
Chicago, Illinois 60604
Phone: (312) 663-3520
Fax: (312) 939-8962
Email: mailbox@preventchildabuse.org
http://www.preventchildabuse.org/
https://www.facebook.com/pages/Prevent-Child-Abuse-America/14893558501
http://www.youtube.com/pcaamerica

Prevent Child Abuse America (PCAA) is committed to promoting legislation, policies, and programs that help prevent child abuse and neglect, support healthy childhood development, and strengthen families. Working with State chapters, PCCA provides leadership to promote and implement prevention efforts at the national and local levels.

PCAA's research arm is the National Center on Child Abuse Prevention Research and Resources http://preventchildabuse. org/resources/. The Center provides a link between research and practice by developing and evaluating prevention strategies, and by disseminating information about child abuse maltreatment and its prevention across the country.

Search Institute

The Banks Building
615 First Avenue NW -- Suite 125
Minneapolis, Minnesota 55413
Phone: (612) 376-8955
Toll-Free: (800) 888-7828

Resources: Child Abuse (continued)

Email: si@search-institute.org
http://www.search-institute.org
https://www.facebook.com/SearchInstitute
https://twitter.com/searchinstitute
http://www.youtube.com/searchinstitute

Search Institute conducts research to identify what children and adolescents need to become caring, healthy, and responsible adults. The Institute also provides resources to apply this knowledge and to motivate and equip others in ensuring young people are valued and that they thrive.

Stop It Now!

351 Pleasant Street
Suite B319
Northampton, Massachusetts 01060
Phone: (413) 587-3500
Toll-Free: (888) 773-8368
Email: info@stopitnow.org
http://www.StopItNow.org
https://www.facebook.com/StopItNow
https://twitter.com/stopitnow
http://www.youtube.com/wecanstopitnow

Stop It Now!® prevents the sexual abuse of children by mobilizing adults, families and communities to take action before a child is harmed. Stop It Now! provides support, information and resources for adults to take responsibility for creating safer communities.

The Full Frame Initiative

308 Main Street
Suite 2A
Greenfield, Massachusetts 01301
Phone: (413) 773-3400
Email: info@fullframeinitiative.org
http://fullframeinitiative.org/

Resources: Child Abuse (continued)

The Full Frame Initiative (FFI) is a national nonprofit organization that works to break cycles of poverty and violence through systems change. FFI has discovered the common DNA among the organizations that effectively serve people with multiple challenges — lasting change occurs when people are supported in the full frame of their lives. Many more organizations would choose to operate with a Full Frame Approach, but they are stymied by rules, regulations and other barriers present throughout the social service system. In partnership with practical visionaries in government, nonprofits, philanthropy and communities, FFI removes systemic barriers to full frame practice, allowing more people and communities to thrive.

ZERO TO THREE

National Center for Infants, Toddlers and Families
2000 M Street NW, Suite 200
Suite 200
Washington, District of Columbia 20036
Phone: (202) 638-1144
Toll-Free: (800) 899-4301
http://www.zerotothree.org
https://www.facebook.com/ZEROTOTHREE

Zero to Three's mission is to promote the healthy development of our nation's infants and toddlers by supporting and strengthening families, communities, and those who work on their behalf. Zero to Three is dedicated to advancing current knowledge, promoting beneficial policies and practices, communicating research and best practices to a wide variety of audiences, and providing training, technical assistance, and leadership development.

Resources: Transgender Issues and Advocacy

American Civil Liberties Union (ACLU)
listing 185 blogs and posts about transgender rights

125 Broad Street, 18th Floor
New York NY 10004
212-549-2500

National Center for Transgender Equality

(202) 642-4542
ncte@transequality.org1133 19th St NW
Suite 302
Washington D.C. 20036
Samuel Lurie, Transgender Training and Advocacy
Tel: 802-453-5370 x2
Fax: 802-453-7096
Email: **info@tgtrain.org**

Transgender Advocacy Network (TAN)

www.transadvocacynetwork.org

Transgender Organizations (listed on Glaad, https://www.
glaad.org/transgender/resources):

Transgender People in Crisis Can Access these Resources:

The Trevor Project's 24/7/365 Lifeline at 866-4-U-TREVOR
(866-488- 7386) or TrevorChat, their online instant
messaging option, or TrevorText, a text-based support option

The National Suicide Prevention Lifeline at 800-273-TALK
(8255)

Trans Lifeline at 877-565-8860

National Center for Transgender Equality (NCTE) (advocacy)

Transgender Law Center (TLC) (legal services and advocacy)

Gender Proud (advocacy)

Sylvia Rivera Law Project (SRLP) (legal services)

Transgender Legal Defense and Education Fund (TLDEF) (legal services)

Massachusetts Transgender Political Coalition (MTPC) (advocacy)

Trans People of Color Coalition (TPOCC) (advocacy)

Resources: Transgender Issues and Advocacy (continued)

Trans Women of Color Collective (TWOCC) (advocacy)

Black Trans Advocacy (advocacy)

Trans Latina Coalition (advocacy)

Gender Spectrum (support for families, trans youth, and educators)

Trans Youth Equality Federation (support for families and trans youth)

Trans Youth Family Allies (TYFA) (support for families and trans youth)

TransTech Social Enterprises (economic empowerment)

SPART*A (advocacy for trans military service members)

<u>Transgender American Veterans Association</u> (advocacy for trans veterans)

<u>https://www.caribbeanequalityproject.org</u>

https://suicidepreventionlifeline.org/media-resources/

National Depression Help.

<u>https://www.nami.org/learn-more/mental-health-conditions /depression/support</u>

CPSIA information can be obtained
at www.ICGtesting.com
Printed in the USA
FFHW010607151019
55476721-61370FF